Changing the Officer Promotion System to Support Unit Focused Stability (UFS)

A Monograph

by

MAJ Sean C. Bernabe

United States Army

School of Advanced Military Studies

United States Army Command and General Staff College

Fort Leavenworth, Kansas

AY 04-05

SCHOOL OF ADVANCED MILITARY STUDIES

MONOGRAPH APPROVAL

MAJ Sean C. Bernabe

Title of Monograph: Changing the Officer Promotion System to Support Unit Focused Stability (UFS)

Approved by:

_____   Monograph Director
J.J Schneider, Ph.D.

_____   Director,
Kevin C.M. Benson, COL, AR   School of Advanced
                                         Military Studies

_____   Director,
Robert F. Baumann, Ph.D.   Graduate Degree
                                         Programs

ABSTRACT

CHANGING THE OFFICER PROMOTION SYSTEM TO SUPPORT UNIT FOCUSED STABILITY (UFS) By Major Sean C. Bernabe, United States Army, 79 pages.

The United States Army is currently implementing a new manning initiative called Unit Focused Stability (UFS). This new personnel program is designed to maximize unit cohesion in Brigade Combat Teams by replacing the Individual Replacement System (IRS) with a unit-centric manning system. While added cohesion within combat units is a positive change for the Army at large, it may bring significant second- and third-order effects that adversely affect Army personnel. The impact of UFS on the officer corps will be especially troublesome.

Unfortunately, the Army has yet to conduct detailed analysis on the side effects of the UFS or to identify the requisite changes across other personnel functions that must complement the switch to UFS. This monograph endeavors to begin such analysis by answering the following research question: Will a change in the officer promotion system help to ensure the long-term success of UFS?

This monograph begins with an analysis of the UFS model and its impact on the officer corps. The examination identifies thirteen friction points for officers in the rank of lieutenant through colonel. These friction points add up to one thing: significant potential for the eventual failure of UFS. As individual officers experience the friction associated with UFS, they will exempt themselves from the program. This paper presents historical evidence to demonstrate that without officer support and participation, unit manning initiatives will eventually fail.

Next, this study examines the officer promotion system to determine its underlying assumptions, their associated implementation principles, and the specific laws and policies that have stemmed from them. The monograph concludes that many of the fundamental assumptions and principles of the officer promotion system are outdated and will contribute to the friction of UFS. Additionally, an exploration into the Defense Officer Personnel Act of 1980 (DOPMA), Department of Defense policy, and Army regulations concludes that any significant change to the foundation of Army officer promotions must be accomplished through changes to Title 10, United States Code.

Finally, this monograph proposes three possible changes to the Army officer promotion system. The first proposal is the adoption of an up-or-stay promotion system. The second option is a new career model with longer career timelines, slower promotions, and wider promotion eligibility zones. The third proposal is the implementation of an event-driven promotion system that divorces promotions from time pressure altogether. Of the three proposals, the second does the most to alleviate the friction points that will be created by UFS.

The monograph concludes that Army must change its officer promotion system to ensure the longevity of UFS and the future health of the officer corps.

TABLE OF CONTENTS

TABLE OF FIGURES

CHAPTER ONE: INTRODUCTION

Since the First World War, the Individual Replacement System (IRS) has been the hallmark of personnel management in the United States Army. The mobilization for the Great War placed a heavy burden on the human resource systems of the nation, and the only way to meet the short-order demands of the war machine was through the rapid development of a personnel system that minimized waste and maximized efficiency. Despite the enormous numbers of men called to service for the war, the Army handled each man as an individual—from initial muster and placement, through training and deployment, to redeployment and discharge.[1] In 1919, Major General H.P. McCain, formerly Adjutant General, explained this need for individual treatment as follows:

> The great war differs from all other wars not merely in the number of individuals involved but even more in the number of technicians demanded. Because of the haste in creating the Army, it was impossible to develop the experts and accordingly those already possessing such technical skill were, when properly assigned, of the greatest value to the new Army.[2]

The need for assignment precision in an already highly specialized Army sparked the development of the soldier-centric Individual Replacement System.

For over eighty years, the IRS has served the Army well. Through peace and war, it has allowed the Army to efficiently man its diverse organizations while simultaneously meeting the personal and professional needs of individual soldiers.[3] Despite its success, the IRS has had no shortage of critics. While maximizing bureaucratic efficiency in a highly specialized army, the

---

[1] U.S. Department of the Army, Committee on Classification of Personnel in the Army, *The Personnel System of the United States Army, Vol. I: History of the Personnel System.* (Washington, D.C.: 1919), 29.

[2] Major General H.P. McCain, "Foreword," in U.S. Department of the Army, Committee on Classification of Personnel in the Army, *The Personnel System of the United States Army, Vol. I: History of the Personnel System.* (Washington, D.C.: 1919), iii.

[3] David Sanders and Mike McGinnis, "Unit Manning the Army's Combat Brigades" (West Point: United States Military Academy Operations Research Center of Excellence, 2003), 6.

personnel turbulence generated by the IRS degrades cohesion and effectiveness of combat units.[4] Army leaders throughout the decades have recognized the inherent conflict between the IRS and unit readiness, and at least a dozen times since World War I, the Army has attempted to migrate from the IRS to a more unit-centric manning system.[5] Invariably, these attempted changes faced significant institutional resistance, and in each case, the Army eventually reverted back to the IRS.[6]

In August 2002, the Secretary of the Army, The Honorable Thomas E. White, announced yet another attempt to break the old manning paradigm. In conjunction with ongoing Army Transformation initiatives, Secretary White directed the formation of a Unit Manning Task Force "to analyze the feasibility of changing how the Army assigns soldiers to combat brigade teams; from the individual replacement system of today to a unit manning system (UMS)."[7] In May 2003, after less than a year of study and analysis, the Chief of Staff, Army (CSA), General Eric Shinseki decided to go forward with the unit manning initiative.[8] Under General Shinseki's successor, General Peter Schoomaker, the unit manning concept was finalized and merged into a formal manning strategy called Unit Focused Stability (UFS). In February 2004, UFS was formally announced to the Army as a critical component to the CSA's Force Stabilization Initiative (see Figure 1).[9]

---

[4] Sanders and McGinnis, 7. Authors cite article by Sean D. Naylor, "Secretary Pushes for Large-Scale Personnel Reform, Sweeping Changes Could Start With Switch to Unit Manning" *Army Times*, 16 September 2002.

[5] Sanders and McGinnis, 8.

[6] Ibid.

[7] Ibid., 7.

[8] Ibid., 41.

[9] *Military Times*. "ARMY Announces Force Stabilization Initiative," February 10, 2004, http://www.military-times.info/article_125.html (accessed 4 August 2004).

Figure 1: Conceptual Diagram of Force Stabilization Initiative[10]

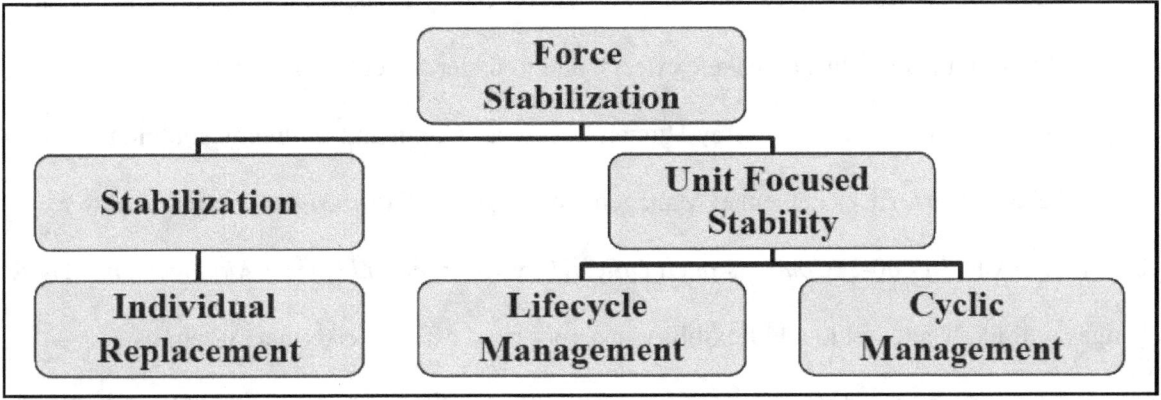

Army leaders prepare to implement UFS according to the master transformation schedule, but they do so with some hesitation and doubt. Intuitively, Army leaders know that unit manning will increase cohesion and combat effectiveness of individual units.[11] However, many leaders also predict that these improvements in unit readiness will come at a high price for the individual officer. In its haste to implement UFS, the Army has only begun to analyze the potential second- and third- order effects of UFS. Even without scientific analysis or advanced computer modeling, the typical officer can deduce one thing: if executed according to its intent, UFS will have a significant impact on professional development, career progression, promotion potential, and command opportunity for the officer corps. Given the Army's poor track record with unit manning initiatives, one must ask several questions: What is to prevent this latest attempt at unit manning from "fizzling out" just like the others did? How can the Army generate enough institutional inertia to ensure the permanence of UFS? What must the Army do to gain the confidence and support of the officer corps in implementing a shift to a unit-centric manning system?

---

[10] U.S. Department of the Army, *AR 600-XX, Force Stabilization (Draft)* (Washington, D.C.: 2004), 7.

Statement of the Problem

Senior Army leaders have recognized that other policy changes must be implemented to enable UFS, to mitigate its negative side effects, and to foster the cultural shift required for its long-term sustainment. The U.S. Army Human Resources Command is already studying potential changes to Officer Personnel Management System 3 (OPMS3) and drafting a new version of DA PAM 600-3, *Commissioned Officer Development and Career Management.* These changes will likely attempt to add flexibility to a very rigid officer personnel system by redefining career paths and standards for branch qualification at each officer grade level.[12] While these changes are a necessary start, they may not go far enough in providing the flexibility required to implement and sustain UFS. What else must the Army do to gain flexibility in officer management and ensure the success of UFS and the future health of the Officer Corps? Perhaps it is time to turn a critical eye on the Officer Promotion System. This monograph attempts to answer the following research question: Will a change in the Officer Promotion System (in conjunction with changes to OPMS3 and associated policies, regulations, and guidelines) help to ensure the long-term success of Unit Focused Stability (UFS)?

Methodology

The purpose of this monograph is to investigate potential changes to the Officer Promotion System that could support the successful implementation of UFS. The investigation uses a three-step methodology. The first step is a thorough analysis of the unit manning concept to determine its historical background, the nature of the UFS model, the realities of its implementation, and its impact on the officer corps. Careful officer career timeline analysis and

---

[11] This assumption has been the subject of recent debates and studies. The Army Research Institute (ARI) is currently studying the implementation of UFS in the 172d SIB to determine the impact of UFS in unit cohesion.

basic career modeling help identify friction points for officers as they implement UFS while operating under the current promotion system. The second step is a study of the officer promotion system to identify its components, legal and regulatory foundations, and underlying assumptions. This analysis identifies specific principles and elements of the promotion system that may conflict with efforts to change the Army manning paradigm. The final step in the methodology is to develop options for changing the officer promotion system to alleviate (or mitigate) the predicted friction points. In the end, this monograph demonstrates that by changing the officer promotion system, the Army can gain the flexibility required to ensure the successful implementation and long-term success of UFS.

Scope and Limitations

Given the spatial constraints of this monograph, the author has narrowed the scope of the investigation in several ways. First, this monograph does not discuss the issues of feasibility, acceptability, or suitability of UFS. This investigation begins with the assumption that unit manning does, in fact, improve unit cohesion and combat effectiveness. From this assumption comes the conclusion that UFS is a good program for the Army and that its successful implementation is critical enough to the Army to warrant radical change in officer management. Thus, this investigation does not question the decision to implement UFS. Rather, it focuses on ways to enable its introduction and sustainment.

Secondly, in discussing officer management, this monograph limits its focus to officers of the Operations Career Field (OPCF) only. The focal point of UFS is the brigade combat team (BCT). Most of the officers in a BCT belong to the OPCF. While UFS will have some impact on officers of the other career fields, its greatest impact will be on members of the OPCF.

---

[12] BG Rhett Hernandez, "OPMS 3 Update," email message to author (and entire officer corps), October 14, 2004.

Thirdly, this monograph considers only the Army aspects of the Officer Promotion System. Current law standardizes many aspects of officer promotions across all services. Each service has unique officer management requirements, and recommended changes to Defense Department promotion policies or to the laws that bound them must eventually be analyzed through a joint lens. However, such analysis will not be conducted in this study.

Finally, this monograph does not address fiscal or budgetary issues related to changes in the way the Army promotes its officers. Granted, any changes to the promotion system may have dramatic financial ramifications. Radical changes may prove financially unfeasible in the long run, but the analysis conducted for this monograph assumes unconstrained fiscal resources. Further analysis by budgetary experts can yield better resolution on the affordability of any changes recommended in this paper.

Organization

This monograph is organized into five chapters. The second chapter addresses the theoretical concept of unit manning, its practical application in the UFS model, and the potential friction points it will generate for the officer corps. The third chapter discusses the officer promotion system in detail to include its principles and assumptions, its statutory and regulatory underpinnings, and its strengths and weaknesses. Chapter Four presents three possible options for change to the current Officer Promotion System. Finally, Chapter Five summarizes the findings of the monograph and provides recommendations for the Army as it moves forward with the transition to UFS.

CHAPTER TWO: UNIT MANNING IN THEORY AND PRACTICE

This chapter explores the concept of unit manning. As a point of departure, it examines the concept of individual replacement—a cornerstone of personnel management throughout the Army's history. Next, this chapter reviews the concept of unit manning in its generic, unconstrained and idealistic form. This sets the stage for an analysis of the UFS Model to determine its objective, intent, implementation rules, and predicted friction points.

Individual Replacement

Before one can understand the concept of unit manning, one must understand the nature of its antithesis—individual replacement. In 1969, the Department of the Army published *Army Regulation 614-1*, in which it describes the U.S. Army Replacement System as "the collective units and activities which are governed by appropriate policies and procedures that are concerned with the efficient flow of personnel into, within, and out of the Army in order to maintain the personnel strength of commands and units."[13] This regulation describes the replacement system as "a base for the contraction or expansion of Army replacement operations under all conditions of peace or war . . . ."[14] AR 614-1 also list four key principles of the replacement system:

> a. The goal is to have the right person in the right job in the right place at the right time. b. The number of personnel in the replacement system must be kept as low as possible in order to maximize effective utilization of personnel. c. Each element of the replacement system must operate in the most effective and efficient manner possible . . . d. Unit strengths normally will be sustained by provision of individual replacements (rather than by unit replacements).[15]

These principles highlight both the individual-centric nature of the U.S. Army's replacement system and its emphasis on efficiency in personnel management. Regulations published since 1969, such as Army Regulation 614-83, *The New Manning System—COHORT Unit Replacement System* (1986), assigned the name Individual Replacement System (IRS) to the Army's way of manning its commands and units.[16]

---

[13] U.S. Department of the Army, *AR 614-1, The U.S. Army Replacement System* (Washington, D.C.: 1969), 1.
[14] Ibid.
[15] Ibid.
[16] U.S. Department of the Army, *AR 600-83, The New Manning System—COHORT Unit Replacement System.* (Washington, D.C.: 1986), 3.

Many factors have driven the Army towards its twentieth century tradition of individual replacement. During the massive mobilizations for the World Wars, Korea, and Vietnam, the Army needed a system that could ensure efficient and flexible utilization of limited and highly-specialized human resources. As technical specialization within the Army increased during the Cold War, so, too, did the need for scientific management of individual soldiers. In his book, *The Unit First: Keeping the Promise of Cohesion*, Christopher C. Straub argues that the individual-centric personnel system is a product of fundamental national values and the American way of life, including "mass production theory of organization, the urge to centralize, the passion for efficiency, and the primacy of the individual."[17]

The IRS has survived so long because it offers significant advantages in personnel management. First, of all possible manning solutions, the IRS is the easiest to manage. With the development and proliferation of computer automation, database technology, and web-based management systems, individual replacement has become an economy of force exercise with one assignment officer managing thousands of individual officers or soldiers.[18] Secondly, the IRS allows efficient manning of the increasingly intricate and specialized structure of the Army. Third, the IRS provides personnel managers the flexibility necessary to address the professional development needs of the individual soldier and officer. Under the IRS, officers and non-commissioned officers are rotated efficiently through critical developmental assignments. As a result, the system creates a large "bench" of leaders with significant breadth of experience who can serve as cadre in the event of mass mobilization. During the Cold War, the creation of a large officer cadre was a key objective of the IRS and its associated personnel management policies. Finally, the IRS also allows for immediate support to emergent missions, such as the creation of

---

[17] Christopher C. Straub, *The Unit First: Keeping the Promise of Cohesion* (Washington, DC: National Defense University Press, 1988), 119.

[18] Based on the author's personal experience as an Assignment Officer at U.S. Total Army Personnel Command (now U.S. Army Human Resources Command), 2000-2002.

new headquarters and units, as was seen in the early days of the Global War on Terrorism with the creation of United States Northern Command and the expansion of Third Army headquarters.

Despite the many positive features of the IRS, its critics highlight several systemic shortcomings. Because of its emphasis on the professional development needs of the individual, the IRS tends to create personnel turbulence within units. The underpinnings of assignment and career equity force personnel changes at inconvenient and inopportune times. Individual management of officers can foster "careerism" and a "ticket-punching" mentality. Perhaps the most scathing indictment of the IRS can be found in Donald Vandergriff's book, *The Path to Victory: America's Army and the Revolution in Human Affairs* (2002). Among other criticisms, Vandergriff argues that the IRS has lowered the "band of excellence" of combat units by forcing huge officer and enlisted turnover rates, especially in the immediate wake of rotations to the Combat Training Centers (CTCs).[19] Throughout the book, Vandergriff derides the personnel system for creating an Army culture of scientific management, of excessive emphasis on career equity, and of individualism vice unit cohesion.[20] Vandergriff's criticism continues even today. In a recent article, Vandergriff illustrates continuing problems of careerism, lack of cohesion, and outdated personnel policies as observed in Operation Iraqi Freedom, and he implicates the IRS as a primary cause:

> The Army personnel system, characterized by the individual replacement system and the Officer/NCO career management system, is the primary cause of these problems. American units and service members have long suffered from the excessive personnel turbulence and careerism caused by the personnel system. The system itself was last codified at the end of World War II. It is a fundamental repudiation of the efforts to take care of and honor the individual service member.
>
> Several Army chiefs have tried to change the system but failed. Opposition to change has historically been centered in the personnel bureaucracy.
>
> Personnel turbulence prevents training continuity, thereby causing low readiness, low proficiency standards and high operations tempo as units strive to overcome organizational defects through long hours of training and frequent training deployments.

---

[19] Donald E. Vandergriff, *The Path to Victory: America's Army and the Revolution in Human Affairs* (Presidio: Presidio Press, 2002), 143.

[20] Ibid., 159.

Careerism leads to micro-management and distrust. It destroys cohesion and turns brothers-in-arms into competitors. The Army can create units that are more ready, and service members who are more satisfied, by changing the personnel system. Use a unit, not an individual, replacement system, and allow officers and NCOs to manage their own careers. A unit rotation system would allow units to keep people together for three or more years and would allow units to develop true competence, as Delta Force soldiers and Navy SEALs have done.[21]

For better or worse, Vandergriff's writings have had a profound influence on senior Army leaders. In fact, his book was one of the catalysts that spurred key Army leaders to examine—for the thirteenth time in the last century—the possibility of implementing a unit manning system.[22]

The Concept of Unit Manning

The concept of unit manning is not new to the United States Army. Prior to World War I, the Army was manned by a regimental system, similar to the famed British Regimental System.[23] Under such a system, all soldiers and most officers served an entire career with the same regiment. Many units contained members from the same family or soldiers from the same geographic area. This close personal connection between soldiers fostered a strong allegiance to the unit and the other members of the regiment. The General Regulations of 1841 recognized the importance of cohesion within these regiments and prescribed that individual squads should be kept together and that personnel transfers should be minimized as much as possible.[24] Despite the countless benefits of this early unit manning system, the significant personnel demands of the

---

[21] Donald A. Vandergriff, "Unit Manning Will Benefit the Many." D.N.I Website at http://www.d-n-i net/fcs/vandergriff unit manning.htm (accessed October 8, 2004).

[22] The author served at U.S. Total Army Personnel Command (PERSCOM) when Vandergriff's book was published and observed its impact on the leaders of PERSCOM. Shortly after publication, Vandergriff was summoned to the offices of the Secretary of the Army, Thomas E. White, and the Army G-1, LTG John M. LeMoyne. Within weeks of these sessions, the Unit Manning Task Force was created to study the feasibility of implementing a unit manning system.

[23] AR 600-83, The New Manning System—COHORT Unit Replacement System. (Washington, D.C.: 1986), 3.

[24] Robert M. Elton, "A Unit Manning System for the Objective Force: Recommendations for Vital Changes in Army Manning Policies." With the collaboration of Joseph Trez. https://www.stabilization.army mil/Research items/manning items, (accessed October 8, 2004) Oct 2002.

Civil War forced both sides to drift away from the concept of unit manning in favor of an individual replacement system.[25] Since then, the concept of unit manning has proven an elusive goal for the U.S. Army.

Unit manning is a "a manning process that reduces turbulence within a unit by synchronizing some portion of the unit's arrivals and departures of personnel."[26] Unit manning makes unit stability and cohesion the primary considerations for all personnel actions. The intent of unit manning is "to set conditions for unit leaders . . . to build cohesive, high performing combat teams by rigorously managing personnel turnover to reduce unit turbulence and stabilize combat units."[27] Unit manning strives to synchronize assignment actions with unit rotations. Such a manning system minimizes personnel turbulence through careful management of all personnel actions to include assignments, schooling, separations, reenlistments, and retirements. Unit manning prioritizes the building of cohesive, combat-effective teams over the professional development and personal wants and needs of individual soldiers and officers. For many, unit manning is the "Holy Grail" of human resource challenges in the Army.[28]

In theory, unit manning is a wonderful solution for maximizing unit cohesion during peacetime training and preparation for deployment. In its pure, theoretical form, a unit manning system assigns all authorized personnel to a given unit for a set, pre-determined period of time (often measured in years). Once assigned to particular positions within the unit, all personnel are "locked in" to those positions for the duration of the manning period. Upon "lock-down," the members of the unit can focus on building cohesive teams at all levels without fear of predicted or unpredicted personnel turnover. All personnel actions—including promotions, professional

---

[25] Ibid.
[26] U.S. Department of the Army, "Task Force Stabilization: Glossary of Terms" https://www.stabilization.army mil/Products_items/TermDefinitions10 mht (accessed July 28, 2004).
[27] David Sanders and Mike McGinnis, "Unit Manning the Army's Combat Brigades" (West Point: United States Military Academy Operations Research Center of Excellence, 2003), 11.

education, separations, transfers, and retirements—are frozen, thus minimizing personnel turbulence.

The unit manning concept is also designed to support wartime replacement operations. As units fill their battle rosters during an initial build phase, they may be assigned a "buffer" of personnel (perhaps an additional ten percent of the normal authorization) to allow for natural attrition and potential wartime casualties. Such losses within the unit are dealt with in one of three ways. First, since the unit is generally manned above authorization, the combat replacement may come from within. Secondly, the unit may wait until an entire squad is combat ineffective and then request a replacement squad. Finally, in rare circumstances, the unit may be forced to request an individual replacement. When a large unit becomes combat ineffective due to mass casualties or vast attrition over time, the entire unit is rotated out of the combat theater and replaced by a like large unit. Thus, the unit manning concept naturally dovetails into a unit rotation concept. In the case of an expeditionary army with multiple, simultaneous overseas missions, the army must synchronize its unit manning cycles with its requirements for unit rotations into overseas theaters.

Such an ideal unit manning system almost eliminates personnel turbulence, thus enabling leaders to maximize horizontal and vertical cohesion within the unit. However, in a modern, bureaucratic army of volunteer soldiers, this idealized unit manning systems quickly becomes unfeasible. Thus, the unit manning models that the U.S. Army and other armies of the world have used (or attempted to use) have all featured significant compromises from the conceptual version. The U.S. Army's current Unit Focused Stability model is no exception.

---

[28] Jamie S. Gayton, "Have We Finally Found the Manning Holy Grail?" *Military Review LXXXIV, No. 2* (Mar-Apr 2004): 17.

The Unit Focused Stability (UFS) Model

As mentioned in the previous chapter, Force Stabilization is one of the Army Chief of Staff's "seventeen immediate focus areas."[29] Force Stabilization has two key components: Stabilization and Unit Focused Stability (UFS). This monograph is focused solely on the latter element.

The UFS model is so new that no formal regulations or manuals have yet been published to explain it in detail. In June 2004, the Army began staffing a draft of *AR 600-xx, Force Stabilization*, but that document is far from final form.[30] Likewise, U.S. Army Human Resources Command has drafted implementation instructions for UFS, but those instructions remain in draft form.[31] Nonetheless, a survey of the draft regulations, recent press releases, and the Department of the Army Force Stabilization Web Site can yield a solid understanding of the UFS model as it will be implemented around the Army.

The UFS model describes how the Army will assign soldiers and officers to brigade combat teams (BCT) or in support of BCTs.[32] The model utilizes two manning strategies: Lifecycle Management and Cyclic Management. The former is designed to synchronize the personnel management cycles with the operational requirements of combat units, specifically, modularized BCTs of Units of Action (UA) and other Modified Table of Organization and Equipment (MTO&E) units where cohesion and combat readiness are critical.[33] The latter is intended to minimize personnel turbulence in the command and control elements above the brigade level and in critical logistics and support outside the combat brigades.

---

[29] U.S. Department of the Army, "Force Stabilization: Key Elements of Force Stabilization" https://www.stabilization.army mil/Overview/Key%20Elements htm (accessed October 8, 2004).

[30] U.S. Department of the Army, *AR 600-XX, Force Stabilization (Draft)*. Washington, D.C.: 2004.

[31] U.S. Army Human Resources Command. *Unit Focused Stabilization Playbook (Final Coordinating Draft)*. Alexandria, VA.: 2004.

[32] "Force Stabilization: Key Elements of Force Stabilization."

[33] *Unit Focused Stabilization Playbook (Final Coordinating Draft)*, 9.

Lifecycle Management has a clear goal: "to synchronize the Soldier's assignment to the operational cycle of the unit, thereby maximizing readiness of the unit through enhanced collective training capability and the resulting unit cohesion."[34] Units managed in accordance with the Lifecycle model will operate on a thirty-six-month operational cycle.[35] This cycle will be divided into three phases: Reset, Train, and Ready (See Figure 2).

Figure 2: Lifecycle Management[36]

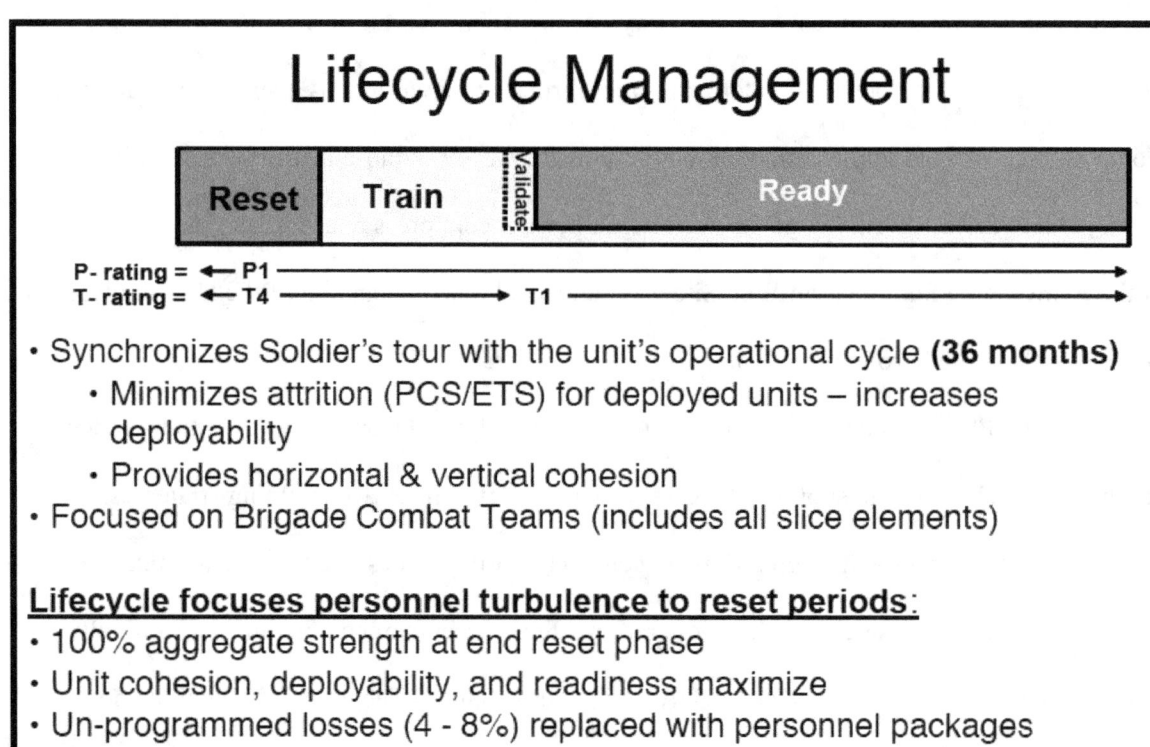

The Reset Phase will last approximately two months. During this phase, the unit simultaneously releases personnel from its previous lifecycle and receives incoming personnel for the current lifecycle. Depending on the particular promotion status and professional development needs of the soldiers in the unit, between twenty-five and forty percent of the unit could remain in

---

[34] Ibid.

[35] Force Stabilization: Key Elements of Force Stabilization."

[36] *Unit Focused Stabilization Playbook (Final Coordinating Draft)*, 10.

place from the previous lifecycle.[37]   At the end of the Reset phase, the unit will have one hundred percent of its authorized personnel, all personnel will be properly in-processed, and all organizational property will be properly transferred. The personnel in a lifecycle unit will be "locked in" to the unit for the duration of the thirty-six-month operational cycle. Naturally, some un-programmed losses may occur, and the draft regulations limit such losses to "critical family needs, soldier misconduct, physical disabilities, or death."[38]

The Train Phase is the critical team-building phase of the Lifecycle Management model. Units in the Train Phase undergo a focused and intense four-month training cycle. This training is designed to build soldier confidence and unit cohesion at all levels through individual and collective training. The Train Phase culminates with a certification exercise at a Combat Training Center (CTC) or a Major Readiness Exercise (MRE) at the unit's home station. Lifecycle Management contributes two key elements towards the effectiveness of this training. First, it ensures that the unit has one hundred percent of authorized personnel prior to the start of training. Secondly, Lifecycle Management minimizes personnel turbulence during the training, thus enabling effective team building.[39]

Following successful certification, the unit then enters the third phase, the Ready Phase. This phase is generally a thirty-month period during which the unit is prepared for worldwide deployment as required by the Army G-3. During periods of employment, the unit rotates as a whole to complete an overseas mission of varying duration. When not deployed, the unit conducts sustainment training to maintain unit proficiency while preparing for the next mission. Since Lifecycle Management virtually eliminates personnel turbulence, the unit "will sustain a higher level of readiness and a narrower band of excellence than in the past."[40] According to the

---

[37] *Unit Focused Stabilization Playbook (Final Coordinating Draft))*, 9.
[38] *AR 600-XX, Force Stabilization (Draft)*, 12.
[39] *Focused Stabilization Playbook (Final Coordinating Draft)*.
[40] *Unit Focused Stabilization Playbook (Final Coordinating Draft)*, 9-10.

model, if units experience a high level of attrition during the course of the lifecycle, the commanders "may request 'package' replacements of soldiers who will in-process and train at the same time, minimizing unit disruption and maximizing unit readiness."[41]

The Human Resources Command *UFS Playbook (Coordinating Draft)* specifies several implementation rules that further define the essence of Lifecycle Management. First, the *Playbook* emphasizes that all rules are "unit centric," that is "Schools, changes of command, and the like are timed to support the unit's operational cycle, rather than detract from it."[42] Second, all enlisted personnel, non-commissioned officers, warrant officers, and officers will arrive at the lifecycle unit during the Reset Phase and remain with the unit for the duration the unit's operational lifecycle.[43] According to the rules, it is incumbent upon the unit commanders to ensure that their initial positioning within the unit allows the proper leadership development.[44] Third, if all implementation rules are enforced properly, the only personnel losses that should occur in a unit under Lifecycle Management should be "unprogrammed losses (i.e., Medical, legal admin, compassionate reassignments, approved exceptions, etc.)," and these losses will be replaced through annual replacement packages.[45] Only under extreme circumstances, will replacements come to a lifecycle unit in a different fashion. Such dire conditions include the loss of a soldier in a "critical, low-density MOS [Military Occupational Specialty]" or if the unit's "aggregate MOS fill falls below 75 percent of authorized."[46] Fourth, Army promotion rules and regulations do not change under Lifecycle Management. Promotion eligibility must be considered when assigning soldier to lifecycle units. If a soldier is promoted while assigned to a BCT, he remains in his current position, thus adhering to the familiar Army principle that allows

---

[41] "Force Stabilization: Key Elements of Force Stabilization."
[42] *Unit Focused Stabilization Playbook (Final Coordinating Draft)*, 10.
[43] Ibid.
[44] Ibid.
[45] Ibid.
[46] Ibid., 10-11.

any soldier to serve "one level above his/her pay grade or two levels below his/her pay grade."[47] If a promotion causes a soldier or officer to be counted as "excess"—that is, above the authorized personnel structure for the unit—the soldier will remain in the unit for the remainder of the lifecycle.[48] Fifth, the Lifecycle Management implementation rules forbid cross-leveling of personnel outside the unit during the lifecycle, and they strongly discourage cross-leveling within the unit.[49] Finally, while the *Playbook* states that the rules for battalion and brigade command tours are currently under review, the policy on command tours for company commanders will not change. Thus, company commanders will still command for twelve to eighteen months in one company, but instead of departing the unit upon completion of command, they will remain with the BCT until completion of the lifecycle.[50]

Lifecycle Management is a significant departure from the Individual Replacement System. At its heart is a complete change in manning philosophy. Under this system, the personal desires and professional needs of the individual soldier and officer are secondary to the need to form, train, and deploy cohesive combat brigades.

The second manning strategy under the umbrella of UFS is Cyclic Management. While cohesion is just as important in combat support (CS) and combat service support (CSS) units as it is in BCTs, it is not feasible to manage all CS and CSS units in accordance with the Lifecycle Management Model. Many command and control, CS, and CSS units are highly specialized and continuously engaged in support missions. Therefore, they do not have the freedom to execute the complete unit "stand-down" associated with the Reset Phase of the Lifecycle Management Model. The developers of UFS found in Cyclic Management a compromise between Lifecycle Management and individual replacement that could provide improved unit cohesion while

---

[47] Ibid., 11.
[48] Ibid.
[49] Ibid.
[50] Ibid.

allowing unimpeded operations for the units. According to the Unit Manning Task Force, the method of "cyclic regeneration is ideally suited for enabling units to recover from losses [of personnel] in the 10 to 30% range where an experienced cadre of veteran soldiers are available to quickly integrate new soldiers into a combat team and conduct individual and collective training."[51]

The goals of Cyclic Management are "to synchronize the Soldier's assignment to the operational cycle of the unit maximizing readiness of the unit through enhanced collective task capability and cohesion while retaining flexibility in personnel management."[52] This is accomplished in two alternating phases: Sustain and Ready (See Figure 3). The Sustain Phase is a pre-determined, one- to two-month period of time during which leader and soldier assignments and personnel moves are executed, un-programmed losses are replaced, and internal personnel cross-leveling is conducted. The Sustain Phase occurs once every twelve months. The second phase is the Ready Phase. This ten- to eleven-month phase is characterized by rapid integration of personnel into existing teams and uninterrupted mission support. Despite the occurrence of an annual Sustain Phase, the goals for individual soldier assignment length remains at thirty-six months (the same goal as for Lifecycle Management).[53]

The implementation rules for Cyclic Management are very similar to the rules for Lifecycle Management. First, soldiers entering and leaving the unit will do so only doing the pre-determined sustain periods. Second, personnel replacements will normally be accomplished through personnel packages that arrive during the Sustain Phase. Individual Replacements will be sent to the unit by exception and generally, only in cases of critical low-density MOS shortages or aggregate MOS fill below seventy-five percent. Guidelines for promotions, internal

---

[51] Sanders and McGinnis, 16.
[52] *Unit Focused Stabilization Playbook (Final Coordinating Draft)*, 15.
[53] Ibid.

cross-leveling, and command managements are identical to the rules under Lifecycle

Management.[54]

Figure 3: Cyclic Management[55]

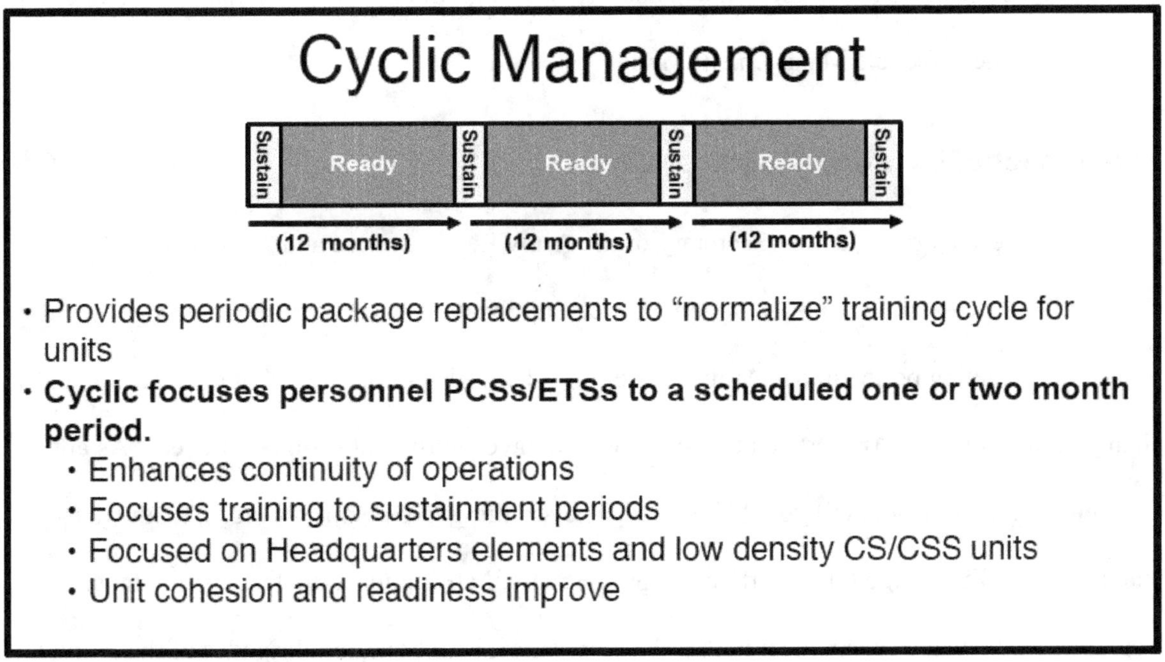

Of the two manning strategies under UFS, Lifecycle Management represents the greater

departure from "business as usual." Lifecycle Management suspends traditional personnel

actions in an effort to provide unit commanders a captive audience for thirty-six months, thereby

creating the conditions for optimized horizontal and vertical cohesion. Under Lifecycle

Management, Human Resources Command uses an ambitious model and strict enforcement rules

to virtually eliminate external personnel turbulence during the thirty-six month lifecycle.

Lifecycle Management will have its greatest impact on combat arms soldiers and Officers of the

Operational Career Field (OPCF)in modularized BCTs. The impact of Cyclic Management will

be much less severe, for the model represents a compromise between the strict Lifecycle

---

[54] *Unit Focused Stabilization Playbook (Final Coordinating Draft)*, 16-17.
[55] Ibid, 15.

Management model and the IRS. Due to its shorter (twelve-month) management cycles, leaders and personnel managers have greater flexibility to make mid-course corrections and to address the individual needs of soldiers, officers, and units. Thus, any discussion about the impact of UFS must inevitably focus on the soldiers and officers in modularized BCTs that are managed according to the Lifecycle Management Model.

The Impact of UFS on the Officer Corps

In a recent article, acting Secretary of the Army Les Brownlee and Army Chief of Staff General Peter Schoomaker call the ongoing Force Stabilization initiatives "the most significant revision in manning policy in our Army's history."[56] They also implicitly recognize that such a change in the complex Army system of systems will have significant residual effects: "As any personnel manager would tell you, 'This changes everything.' And so it should."[57] But what exactly does UFS change for the officer corps? How will UFS impact the leaders that must implement Lifecycle Management within the companies, battalions, and brigades of the Army?

The Army has conducted little formal modeling to predict the second- and third- order effects of UFS for the officer corps. The Unit Manning Task Force used a formal scheduling model to determine the strategic feasibility of implementing a unit manning system while simultaneously meeting worldwide deployment requirements and conducting multiple Transformation initiatives.[58] Beyond that, the only modeling the task force conducted was the identification of "friction points" by analyzing plans to implement Lifecycle Management in the 172nd Stryker Brigade Combat Team. The execution timeline for UFS has been so ambitious that even the analysts of Human Resources Command have done little more than "mental

---

[56] Les Brownlee and Peter J. Schoomaker, "Serving a Nation at War: A Campaign Quality Army with Joint and Expeditionary Capabilities," *Parameters* XXXIV, No. 2 (Summer 2004) 16.
[57] Ibid.
[58] Sanders and McGinnis, 22.

modeling" of the long-term effects.[59] Nonetheless, by comparing current officer career timelines with the UFS model, one can predict general friction points. The following is an analysis of the friction points that develop when combat arms officers under current personnel management parameters enter a BCT under the Lifecycle Management Model.

Friction Points for Lieutenants

Upon accession into the Army, all lieutenants go to training bases for Initial Entry Training (IET). Depending upon the individual officer's branch, prior experience, and required additional schooling (such as Airborne School, Ranger School, Bradley Leader's Course, etc.), the officer will spend between six and eighteen months at the training base before arrival at his first duty station.[60] Combat arms officers—who make up the majority of the junior officers in a BCT—tend towards the longer initial training timelines. Given that the current promotion timeline to First Lieutenant is twenty-four months, the officer will arrive at the BCT with only six to twelve months of time remaining as a second lieutenant. This "time crunch," in and of itself is not a significant concern. However, when combined with the other constraints of Lifecycle Management, the time crunch becomes a friction point.

While awaiting the determination of initial assignment upon completion of IET, lieutenants will encounter another friction point—the reduction in assignment options and the immediate division of the officer population into "haves" and "have nots." Upon completion of IET, lieutenants will be assigned to a BCT that is executing the Reset Phase of the Lifecycle Management Model. Since readiness concerns dictate that all BCTs of the Army cannot be in the Reset Phase at the same time, not all units will be viable assignment options for the young officer. Secondly, based on current accession levels and unit structure, not all lieutenants will be able to

---

[59] C. Neil Fulcher, Chief, Distribution, Development, and Programs Branch, Officer Personnel Management Directorate, U.S. Army Human Resources Command (phone interview, September 28, 2004)
[60] Ibid.

go to BCTs.[61] Many will be forced to fill lieutenant requirements in non-MTO&E units. Thus, officer assignment preference is subverted by the operational requirements of the Army—not surprising in a unit manning system that dissolves the assumption of the primacy of the individual.

While officer preference is a significant concern for the officer corps, a more substantial issue upon arrival to the BCT is the issue of initial duty positions within the BCT. Under the current officer career timelines, all lieutenants assigned to the BCTs must be new accessions coming out of IET. All incoming lieutenants will be second lieutenants, and except for the small percentage of them with prior enlisted service, most will have the same level of experience. The lieutenant positions within the BCT vary in scope and responsibility and thus, call for varying degrees of experience and maturity. Traditionally, the entry-level duty position for a lieutenant is rifle or tank platoon leader. After gaining experience in this initial position and demonstrating potential for increased responsibility, lieutenants are later moved to specialty platoon leader positions (support platoon leader, mortar platoon leader, scout platoon leader, etc.), to company executive officer positions, or to assistant staff officer positions. Lifecycle Management does not support the requirement for cascading experience among lieutenants.[62] Thus, the Lifecycle Management Model presents a significant dilemma for commanders: how does one fill all the critical lieutenant positions within a brigade if all incoming lieutenants are inexperienced second lieutenants straight out of IET? This dilemma represents another friction point for lieutenant management under UFS.

The challenges of junior officer management are further exacerbated when considering the current timeline for promotion to captain. Under the current rules, officers are promoted to

---

[61] Ibid.

[62] U.S. Department of the Army, "Force Stabilization: Leader Information Briefing" https://www.stabilization.army mil/Briefings/Ldr%20Info%20Brief.ppt (accessed October 8, 2004).

captain between 36 and 42 months of service.[63] Thus, all the lieutenants who enter a BCT during

the Reset Phase will be promoted to Captain at some time during the thirty-six month Lifecycle.

The authors of the implementation rules for the Lifecycle Model recognize this, dismissing it by

invoking the "One-Up, Two-Down Rule," and stating that "there is nothing inherently wrong

with a captain who is a company executive officer. . . ."[64] While a combat arms company can

certainly function with three captain platoon leaders, a captain as company executive officer, and

a captain as company commander, there is something decidedly dysfunctional about this

arrangement. The author experienced a similar situation in the late Nineties as a company

commander in First Infantry Division. In 1999, the Army changed the pin-on date for captain

from forty-two months to thirty-six months. This policy change meant that most of the company

executive officers were promoted to captain during their tenure. The author's company

functioned with a captain company commander and a captain executive officer, but the situation

presented certain challenges. What was once a clear senior-subordinate relationship became

more familiar as the commander and his "second-in-command" wore the same rank. The Officer

Evaluation System presented a greater challenge. Upon promotion, the captain executive officer

joined a new Officer Evaluation Report (OER) rating scheme. Although he had little interaction

with the brigade commander, his promotion moved him into the population of captains who were

senior rated by the brigade commander. Granted, professional officers worked through this

friction, but not without some discomfort, angst, and concern.

Another friction point for lieutenants involves the inability of these junior officers to gain

breadth of assignment experience during the course of a BCT's lifecycle. The Lifecycle

Management model attempts to eliminate external personnel turbulence and strongly encourages

commanders to minimize internal turbulence caused by changes in duty positions:

---

[63] This pin-on point has moved several times in the last eight years from a high of 48 months in
1996 to a low of 36 months in 1999.

Lifecycle managed personnel will not be cross-leveled outside of the unit until conclusion of the unit Lifecycle (i.e. the next Reset phase). Movement of personnel within the Lifecycle unit is at the discretion of the unit commander. However, Force Stabilization strongly discourages internal turbulence that would impact on unit readiness levels. Crew, team, subunit readiness levels could be affected when making internal personnel moves. The brigade and battalion level command teams must consider these factors when seeking the right balance between professional development needs of Soldiers and mission.[65]

Commanders who interpret the intent of unit manning in its strictest sense may leave a lieutenant in the same duty position for the entire three-year lifecycle. Commanders who seek more of a balance between traditional professional development of the individual officer and the desire for unit cohesion will still find themselves hamstrung. They will lack the flexibility to give junior officers a variety of professional experiences during the course of the BCT's lifecycle. Under Lifecycle Management, the BCT is nearly a closed system. New officers will enter the unit only in response to un-programmed personnel losses, and they will join the unit as part of the annual package replacement. Without a steady flow of incoming lieutenants, the battalion commanders will have a limited ability to move lieutenants through an assignment pattern of progressive responsibility. In order to allow a rifle or tank platoon leader to transition to a company executive officer position, one of the company executive officers will be forced to regress to a platoon leader position. Thus, in the interest of professional development of one officer, a second officer will be forced to backpedal to jobs of reduced scope and diminished responsibility.

Friction Points for Captains

The friction points for Captains center around one professional experience: the opportunity to command a company within a BCT. Under the Lifecycle Management Model, not every officer will get the chance to command in a BCT. Those who do will forfeit other

---

[64] *Unit Focused Stabilization Playbook (Final Coordinating Draft)*, 11.
[65] *Unit Focused Stabilization Playbook (Final Coordinating Draft)*, 11.

developmental opportunities within the battalions and brigade. Finally, the Army as a whole will produce fewer branch-qualified captains, which will impact on other Army programs.

As a BCT fills its ranks during the Reset Phase, it can expect to receive about thirty-one combat arms captains to fill its command and staff positions.[66] Each of these officers will be a recent graduate of the Captains Career Course, with about fifty-four months time-in-service.[67] The typical BCT under Limited Conversion Division (LCD) XXI structure has only fourteen companies (nine line companies, four headquarters companies, and a reconnaissance troop). Obviously, it is physically impossible for all officers to command a company at the beginning of the lifecycle. Again, the brigade commander faces a dilemma: whom does he choose for company command when all incoming officers have approximately the same level of experience and when none have had the opportunity to demonstrate their command potential?

The closed Lifecycle system creates another friction point for combat arms captains. If the Brigade Commander elects to generate internal turbulence by changing company commanders eighteen months (halfway) into the lifecycle, he may not able to give every captain a command opportunity. Under the LCD XXI structure, there are eighteen staff positions for combat arms captains and fourteen command positions. With a mass changeover in company commanders at the lifecycle midpoint, there will still be three captains who will not have the opportunity to command. Of course, it is unrealistic to believe that a brigade commander would elect to change every company commander in his brigade at the same time. Such a move would generate such overwhelming personnel turbulence that the brigade would undoubtedly experience a dangerous

---

[66] Modified Table of Organization and Equipment (MTOE) for 2d Brigade, 1st Infantry Division (UIC: WAMLAA, DOC #87042LE103, EDATE 16 OCT 05); 1st Battalion, 26th Infantry (UIC: WAM3AA, DOC# 07245LE101, EDATE 16 OCT 05); 1st Battalion, 18th Infantry (UIC WAM4AA, DOC# 07245LE101, EDATE 16 OCT 05); 1st Battalion, 77th Armor (UIC WAM8AA, DOC# 17375LE101, EDATE 16 OCT O5); and E Troop, 4th Armor (UIC WJHBAA, DOC # 17083FE101), EDATE: 16 OCT 05), available at https://webtaads.belvoir.army.mil/usafmsa/ . The documents show an authorization of 6 combat arms captains for HHC BDE, 8 combat arms captains for each battalion, and one combat arms captain in the brigade reconnaissance troop for a total of 31 combat arms captains in the brigade.

dip in readiness. Thus, in reality, there would be more than three captains who would not get the opportunity to command a company. Structure changes could alleviate some of the friction for captains. If the new Units of Action have more companies in each battalion and more battalions in each brigade, then it seems there may be increased opportunity for company command. However, this increase would be tempered by the fact that these "new command opportunities" will likely not be the result of "new structure" but rather, re-allocated structure. Thus, while local command opportunity may increase in one BCT, the aggregate command opportunity throughout the Army will remain unchanged.

Reduced command opportunity for captains leads to another friction point: a reduction in branch-qualified captains for the Army at large. Department of the Army Pamphlet 600-3, *Commissioned Officer Development and Career Management* defines branch qualification for most captains as eighteen months (plus or minus six months) in company, battery, or troop command.[68] Assuming this definition remains constant, the Lifecycle Management system will yield about one-third fewer branch-qualified captains each year.[69] Under current Army structure, branch-qualified captains fill critical positions such as Small Group Instructors (SGIs), Observer-Controllers at the CTCs, company commanders in United States Army Recruiting Command (USAREC), and in Active Component/Reserve Component (AC/RC) assignments. The Army already struggles to fill all of the positions designated for branch-qualified captains. Unit Focused Stability will exacerbate this problem.

---

[67] Based on the author's calculations: 12 months Initial Entry Training + 36 months in BCT lifecycle + 6 months Captains Career Course = 54 months Time In Service.

[68] U.S. Department of the Army, *DA Pam 600-3, Commissioned Officer Development and Career Management* (Washington, D.C.: 1998), 10.

[69] Fulcher.

Friction Points for Majors

The UFS Playbook offers no specific guidance on the management of majors. Strict interpretation of the rules that apply to all soldiers dictates that majors will be assigned into BCTs during the Reset Phase and will be locked-in to a duty position for the duration of the lifecycle. Under this strict management system, majors will not execute the traditional rotation between branch qualifying jobs (i.e. between Battalion Operations Officer and Battalion Executive Officer). Even if the Brigade Commander decides to move majors around within BCT to provide a broader professional experience for them, the BCT under Lifecycle Management remains a closed system. Barring casualties and other un-programmed losses, the majors that begin the lifecycle remain with the unit for the full, thirty-six-month lifecycle, and no additional majors join the unit until the next Reset Phase. The closed system actually benefits the majors assigned to the BCT; most will enjoy thirty-six months of time in branch-qualifying positions—significantly more than the current average of less than twenty-four months.[70] However, the closed system also produces two significant friction points for majors outside the BCT.

The first critical friction point involves the majors outside the brigade awaiting their opportunity to serve in branch-qualifying duty positions. Those majors who are not fortunate to be assigned to a BCT immediately will have to serve elsewhere while awaiting an opportunity to join a BCT during its Reset Phase. Depending on the number of BCTs on that particular post, the stagger between their lifecycles, and the number of majors in the queue, a major could wait as long as thirty-six months for the opportunity to serve in his critical, branch-qualifying position. Although such an officer would certainly be gainfully employed while awaiting his turn, the delay in branch qualification puts him at risk for promotion to lieutenant colonel. According to

---

[70] Infantry Branch, OPMD, Human Resources Command, "Infantry Branch Brief, CGSC Class AY 04-05," (Briefing, Command and General Staff College, Fort Leavenworth, KS, August 17, 2004). Those officers selected by the FY04 LTC Board had an average of 15.3 months BQ time as Majors. Those officers selected by the FY05 BN Command Board had an average of 26.9 months BQ time as Majors.

current law, majors are in the Primary Zone (PZ) of consideration for promotion to lieutenant colonel when they have sixteen years of service.[71] Most majors complete Intermediate Level Education between their twelfth and fourteenth years of service.[72] Thus, the average major has between two and four years to complete his branch-qualification prior to his PZ board for lieutenant colonel. Those majors who go straight to a BCT upon completion of ILE will complete branch qualification in plenty of time for the PZ consideration. Those majors who are not lucky enough to get straight to a BCT will experience a significant "time crunch."

A superficial way for the Army to relieve this friction point is to change the definition of branch qualification. *DA Pam 600-3* defines branch qualification for Operations Career Field officers as "24 months in a branch-qualifying assignment."[73] For infantry majors, it further defines branch qualification as "a combined 24 month experience" as battalion executive officer (XO), battalion operations officers (S3), or brigade XO/S3.[74] For armor majors, it reduces the time standard to "eighteen months plus or minus six months."[75] The Army could change the time standard for branch-qualification, and it could expand the list of duty positions that qualify as branch-qualifying. However, such a solution is dangerous in that it produces a corps of senior majors and junior lieutenant colonels who lack critical developmental experiences. A better, more long-term solution must find a way to relieve the time pressure for majors who strive to meet critical career "gates" prior to competing for promotion.

The second friction point for majors outside the BCT stems from the fact that the closed Lifecycle Management system produces fewer branch-qualified majors over the course of its lifecycle than a traditional brigade would produce in an equivalent period. Under the IRS, a typical combat brigade would produce as many as twenty-one branch-qualified majors in a six-

---

[71] *DA Pam 600-3, Commissioned Officer Development and Career Management*, 21.
[72] Ibid., 38.
[73] Ibid., 11.
[74] Ibid., 35.

year period (see Figure 4). Under Lifecycle Management, a BCT would produce only fourteen BQ majors after two lifecycles (six years) (see Figure 5). Current Army structure has significant demands for branch-qualified, combat arms majors, including critical positions at Combat Training Centers, in Active Component/Reserve Component (AC/RC) units, and on the Army Staff. There is also a significant requirement for branch-qualified majors in joint assignments, as mandated by the Goldwater-Nichols Act of 1986. Since the Army's production of branch-qualified majors will drop by about one third under UFS, the Army will have to do one of two things: either reduce requirements for majors or send non-branch-qualified majors to these critical positions. The latter option (probably the more likely) will exacerbate the "time crunch" for these officers as they attempt to branch-qualify before their lieutenant colonel promotion board.

---

[75] Ibid.,42.

Figure 4: Production of Branch-Qualified (BQ) Majors Under IRS

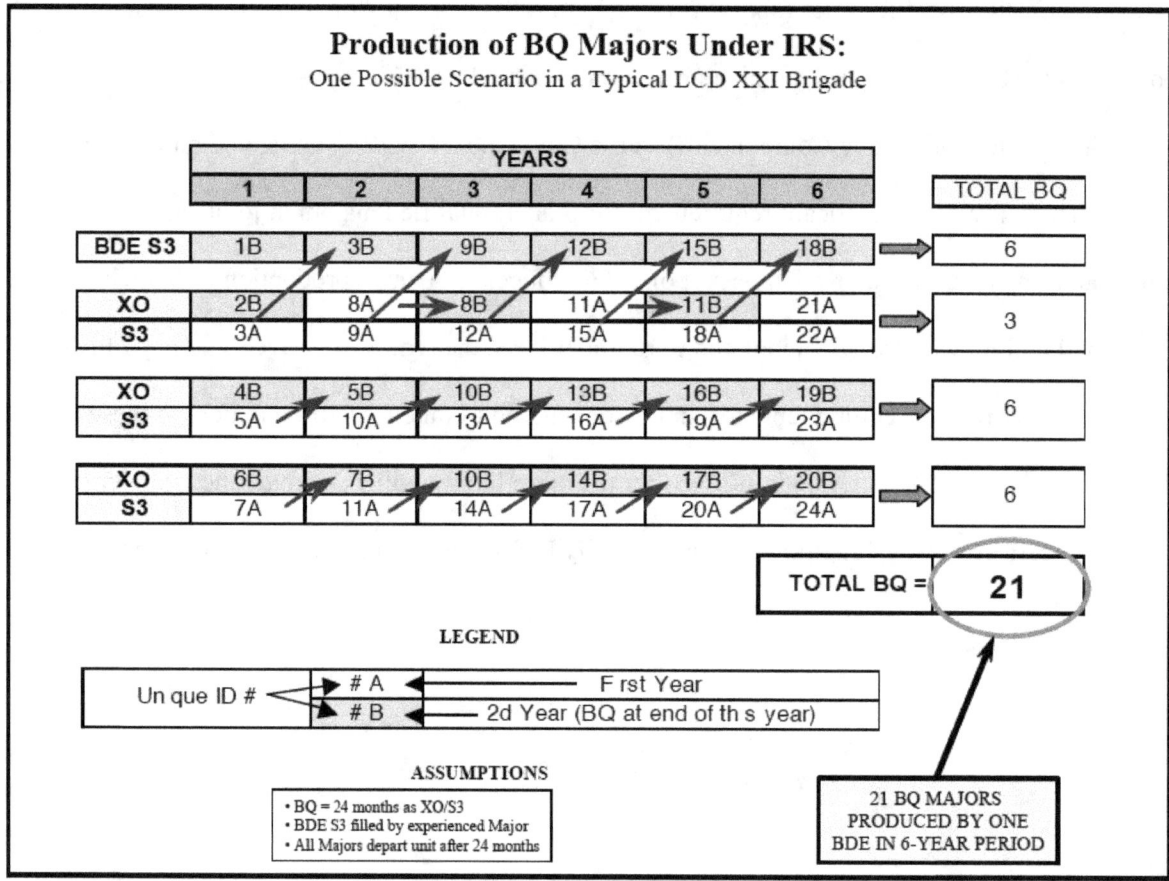

Production of BQ Majors Under IRS:
One Possible Scenario in a Typical LCD XXI Brigade

	YEARS						TOTAL BQ
	1	2	3	4	5	6	
BDE S3	1B	3B	9B	12B	15B	18B	6
XO	2B	8A	8B	11A	11B	21A	3
S3	3A	9A	12A	15A	18A	22A	
XO	4B	5B	10B	13B	16B	19B	6
S3	5A	10A	13A	16A	19A	23A	
XO	6B	7B	10B	14B	17B	20B	6
S3	7A	11A	14A	17A	20A	24A	

TOTAL BQ = **21**

LEGEND

Unque ID# → # A ← First Year
B ← 2d Year (BQ at end of ths year)

ASSUMPTIONS
- BQ = 24 months as XO/S3
- BDE S3 filled by experienced Major
- All Majors depart unit after 24 months

21 BQ MAJORS PRODUCED BY ONE BDE IN 6-YEAR PERIOD

Figure 5: Production of Branch-Qualified (BQ) Majors Under Lifecycle Management

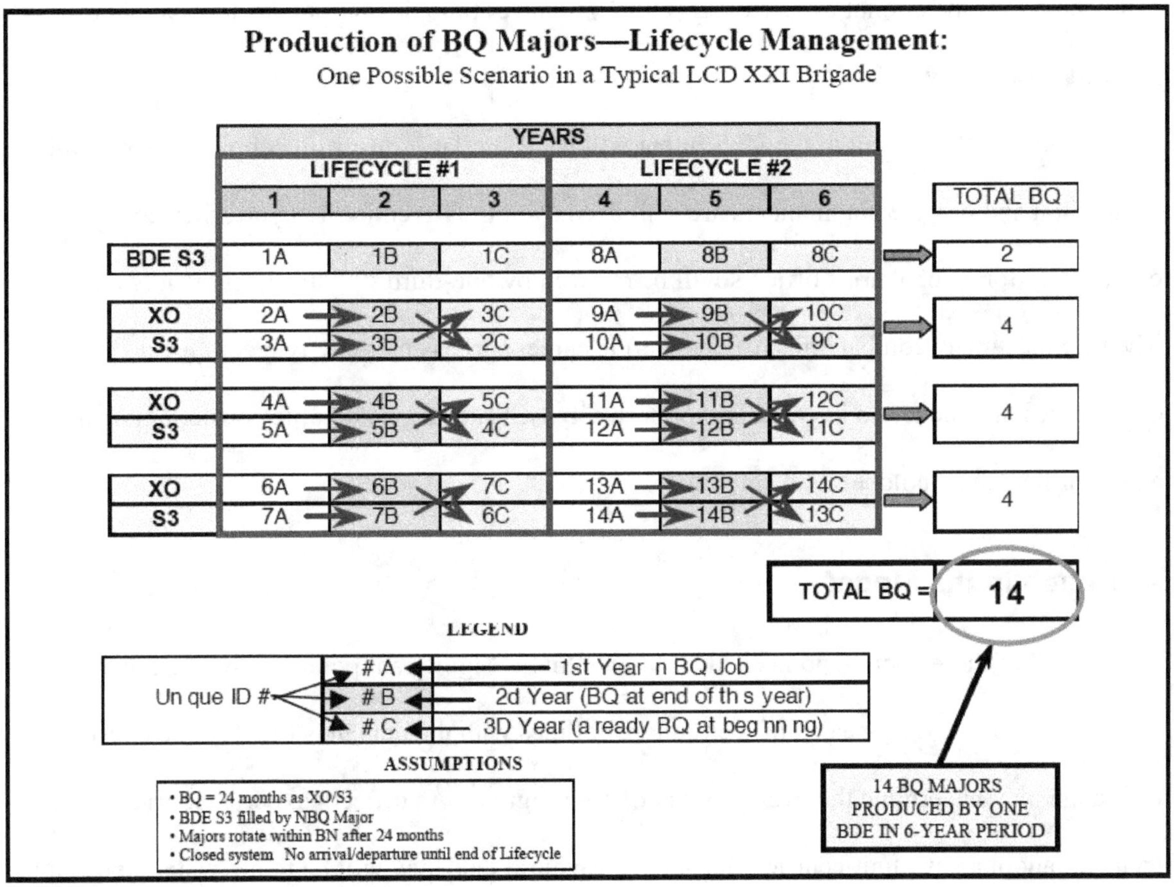

Production of BQ Majors—Lifecycle Management:
One Possible Scenario in a Typical LCD XXI Brigade

	YEARS						TOTAL BQ
	LIFECYCLE #1			LIFECYCLE #2			
	1	2	3	4	5	6	
BDE S3	1A	1B	1C	8A	8B	8C	2
XO	2A → 2B	3C		9A → 9B	10C		4
S3	3A → 3B	2C		10A → 10B	9C		
XO	4A → 4B	5C		11A → 11B	12C		4
S3	5A → 5B	4C		12A → 12B	11C		
XO	6A → 6B	7C		13A → 13B	14C		4
S3	7A → 7B	6C		14A → 14B	13C		

TOTAL BQ = **14**

14 BQ MAJORS PRODUCED BY ONE BDE IN 6-YEAR PERIOD

LEGEND

Unique ID # →
- # A ← 1st Year in BQ Job
- # B ← 2d Year (BQ at end of this year)
- # C ← 3D Year (already BQ at beginning)

ASSUMPTIONS
- BQ = 24 months as XO/S3
- BDE S3 filled by NBQ Major
- Majors rotate within BN after 24 months
- Closed system. No arrival/departure until end of Lifecycle

Friction Points for Lieutenant Colonels and Colonels

The biggest issue for lieutenant colonels and colonels under UFS involves command opportunity. Currently, senior Army leaders are undecided about changes in command policy that may results from implementation of UFS.[76] Prior to the Global War on Terrorism, Army policy limited battalion and brigade command tours to twenty-four months. During Operation Enduring Freedom and Operation Iraqi Freedom, senior leaders decided to stabilize commanders for the duration of overseas deployment. As a result, many commanders remained in their positions for well over twenty-four months. While this policy was infinitely beneficial for the units involved, the second-order effect was a longer command queue for lieutenant colonels and colonels in the Operational Career Field (OPCF).[77] Over time, longer queues translate into reduced opportunity.

Strict enforcement of the UFS intent will have similar impacts on command opportunity. If battalion and brigade commanders are stabilized for a BCT's entire lifecycle, then command opportunity for combat arms officers will be reduced by one-third.[78] This decrement is far from trivial. Since many combat arms officers define career success by these two command experiences, the reduction in command opportunity will cause considerable consternation and angst for lieutenant colonels and colonels.

A Breach in the Model

All of these friction points add up to one thing—significant potential for the eventual failure of UFS. As deep-seated officer culture collides with the demands of UFS, the resistance to change may undermine the overall intent of the program. As officers experience friction while trying to adopt a new, unit-centric mindset, their natural tendency will be to alleviate the friction in one of two ways: either by re-defining their own priorities and definitions of career success, or by inventing informal "work-arounds" to regain the status quo of the old personnel management paradigms. Given the Army's history of failed unit manning initiatives, the latter is far more likely.

---

[76] U.S. Department of the Army, "Force Stabilization: Frequently Asked Questions" https://www.stabilization.army mil/faqs.htm (accessed October 8, 2004).

[77] The author personally knows officers on both sides of this equation. The officers in the queue for battalion and brigade command spent extra time (at least a year in most cases) on Army, corps, or division staffs awaiting their opportunity to take command.

[78] The current system changes out 35 tactical infantry battalions every odd year, and 35 tactical infantry battalions every even year, for a total or 70 battalions every two years (see "Infantry Branch Brief"). Under UFS, the 70 tactical battalions will be changed out over a three-year cycle—23 in the first year, 23 in the second year, and 24 in the third year. Thus, each year group will compete for only 23 battalion commands—which is only 66% of the 35 command opportunities available every year under the current system (23/35=.66).

The design of the UFS model is very telling, for it leaves just enough leeway for commanders to violate the overall intent of the program. The *UFS Playbook* recognizes two types of personnel turbulence. According the draft publication, external turbulence "refers to personnel moves into or out of the unit-under-consideration," and "will be managed by HQDA [Headquarters, Department of the Army]."[79] The other form of personnel turbulence is internal turbulence, described in the *Playbook* as follows:

> *Internal Turbulence* involves personnel moves internal to the unit-under-consideration and will be managed by the unit commander. The Army's individual replacement system, 'focuses on personal career development and desires, rather than Army needs and readiness.' While each internal change in position causes churn and turbulence, internal moves create less friction and have less impact on unit cohesion than external turbulence. Under Force Stabilization, the unit manages internal turbulence that would impact on unit readiness levels. Crew, team, subunit readiness levels could be affected when making internal personnel moves. The brigade and battalion level command teams must consider these factors when seeking the right balance between professional development needs of Soldiers and mission.[80]

Thus, while the UFS Model strongly discourages internal changes of duty position for the sake of professional development, it allows battalion and brigade commanders the flexibility to execute such moves if deemed necessary in the interest of professional development for individual soldiers and officers. Unfortunately, this policy allowance, when combined with a pervasive culture of individuality, "careerism," and equity, becomes a slippery slope towards program failure.

Proactive commanders and personnel managers around the Army are already preparing to implement UFS according to the Army's modularity schedule. The current plan implements Lifecycle Manning incrementally between Fiscal Year 2004 (FY04) and FY09.[81] However, as

---

[79] *Unit Focused Stabilization Playbook (Final Coordinating Draft*, 19.

[80] Ibid.

[81] U.S. Department of the Army, Human Resources Command. "Life Cycle Management." Briefing Slide. Alexandria, VA.: 2004. The current schedule implements Lifecycle Management in three BCTs in FY04, six BCTs in FY05, ten in FY06, thirteen in FY07, five in FY08, and two in FY09

these leaders study the details of the program and its implementation rules, they are already finding shortcuts and exceptions-to-policy that undermine the intent of the system.

In September 2004, the author conducted informal interviews with Deputy Chiefs of Staff G-1, officer strength managers, and chiefs of staff from four different divisions and two corps headquarters. When asked about plans to implement Lifecycle Management, most indicated that for the officer corps, personnel management under the new system would be "business as usual." When asked, "What effect will Lifecycle Management have for majors attempting to complete branch-qualification?" the common answer from officer managers was, "there will be no effect." One senior officer stated, "We cannot afford to stop career progression for majors just to implement Lifecycle." Personnel managers in I Corps recently secured approval from the Vice Chief of Staff, Army (VCSA) for an alternate version of lifecycle management that will "ease the pain" of transitioning to the proposed thirty-six month lifecycles. [82] This alternate version represents a hybrid between the Lifecycle Management Model and Cyclic Management. It reduces the lifecycle to twenty-four months, and it schedules the replacement of certain officers and soldiers after the first year of stabilization. Obviously, this hybrid will fall well short of the stated objectives for UFS.

Some might contend that any cohesion is better than no cohesion. Others may argue that Lifecycle Management is not intended to stabilize the officer corps; rather, it is aimed solely at non-commissioned officers and enlisted soldiers. If this is true, then the Army has failed to learn the lessons of its last attempt at unit manning—the Cohesion, Operational Readiness, and Training (COHORT) Unit Manning System of 1986. Despite countless studies, pilot programs, and policy-changes designed to make COHORT succeed, the program dissolved after a few years. The COHORT program failed for a variety of reasons, including the fact that it was not implemented universally across the Army. It did not apply to all combat units of the Army, so it quickly created two Army's—the "haves" and the "have nots." Another significant reason for the failure of COHORT was the fact that it did not apply to officers:

> The final mistake that prevented COHORT from reaching its full potential was the decision not to include officers in the COHORT cycles. General [Edward C.] Meyer reached a compromise with personnel managers and the majority of senior officers who said that including officers in the full COHORT cycle would be unfair. Combat arms officer locked into the unit rotation until completion would fall behind as others took advantage of career-enhancing schools and assignments or advanced civilian schooling. Because of this concern, COHORT remained focused at the enlisted level. . . Adherence to a unit system in which officers were "stuck" in a unit cycle for three years was likely to place them at a disadvantage when it came time for promotion and school selections. Business-style career progression and the drive to reward ambition once again overrode combat readiness and effectiveness.[83]

If the Army allows de facto officer exemption from UFS, then the program may meet its demise in the same way COHORT did.

Thus, the question remains: can the Officer Corps overcome decades of institutional programming and bureaucratic inertia to make the shift to a unit manning system? Will the Army officer culture undermine UFS before is has a chance to succeed? How can the officer corps gain some measure of flexibility and maneuver space in its career progression models so that its members are not forced to choose between personal career success and unit cohesion? Perhaps a study of the officer promotion system will yield some answers.

CHAPTER THREE: ANALYSIS OF THE OFFICER PROMOTION SYSTEM

For most Army officers, the promotion system is a "black box." Few have read the laws and policies that form the structure of the system, and still fewer have taken the time to consider the assumptions upon which this structure is built.

---

[82] MAJ Alan Kellogg, I Corps Strength Manager, email to author, October 21, 2004.
[83] Vandergriff, *The Path to Victory*, 131-132.

The purpose of this chapter is to explore the U.S. Army officer promotion system to determine its underlying assumptions, their associated principles of implementation, and the specific laws and policies that have stemmed from them. Many of these assumptions and principles are products of the post-Second World War drawdown, and as such, they have been pillars of officer management for over fifty years. A re-examination of the assumptions of the officer promotion system is essential to the successful implementation of UFS. Such an examination must begin with a brief review of history.

A Brief History of the Officer Promotion System

Despite trends in Europe, the United States did not embrace the idea of a standing officer corps until the early nineteenth century. The experience of the American Revolution left lawmakers with a strong faith in the militia, a deep distrust of standing armies, and a profound aversion to the idea of a professional officer class. In 1802, Congress authorized the establishment of the United States Military Academy at West Point and thus, paved the way for a regular army officer corps that would be populated through an annual flow of officer cohorts.[84]

Officer promotion in the nineteenth century was dominated by a seniority system. Upward mobility was possible only when vacancies arose at higher grades. Without a mechanism to force the departure of senior officers, such vacancies were rare. The seniority system lead to widespread stagnation in the officer corps. Frustrated with the limited upward mobility, many disgruntled junior officers resigned, and this eventually prompted a minor reform effort in 1836.[85] Despite efforts to compensate officers for the lack of promotion opportunity and to institute a retirement system, stagnation in the officer corps persisted. The Army entered the

---

[84] Bernard Rostker et al., *The Defense Officer Personnel Management Act of 1980: A Retrospective Assessment* (Santa Monica: Rand, 1993), 75.
[85] Ibid., 76.

Civil War with an aged and undersized officer corps that was wholly unprepared to lead the newly-expanded Army.

From the Civil War through the First World War, officer promotion was characterized by variations on the seniority theme. In the wake of the Civil War, officers were generally promoted based on seniority and vacancies within their own regiments. Congressional action in 1890 created a semi-centralized promotion system whereby officers below the grade of brigadier general were promoted within their own branches or departments. The legislation limited the strength for each grade within each branch, and it required junior officers (major and below) to take examinations for promotion.[86] The Army embraced this "seniority-within-branch" promotion system up through mobilization for the First World War.[87]

During the Interwar Period, the Army's promotion system was strictly a seniority system for officers in the grade of colonel and below. Laws dictated strict limits at each grade level, and when a vacancy developed at a certain grade, the most senior officer at the lower grade was promoted. While this system was equitable and easily managed, it produced stagnation and limited upward mobility for the most capable officers. Common under this system were "14-year-in-grade lieutenants and 52-year-old lieutenant colonels."[88] Despite legislative attempts to add vitality to the officer corps, the Army entered World War II with an aged officer corps that was ill-prepared for the rigors of global war.

Beginning in 1940, Army Chief of Staff General George C. Marshall undertook a program to purge the officer corps by eliminating over-aged officers and rapidly promoting capable junior officers. The Army Vitalization Act of July 1941 provided Marshall authority for continued purges of the old and inefficient members of the officer corps.[89] Through painstaking

---

[86] Ibid., 79.
[87] Ibid., 84.
[88] Ibid., 88.
[89] Ibid., 88-89.

management in the early months of World War II, Marshall culled the officer corps, forcing the

retirement of those officers who were of limited value to a war-time army and disregarding the

normal seniority rules to find the best officers for critical command positions throughout the

force. During the war, promotions through the rank of lieutenant colonel were generally

decentralized, that is, they were left to the discretion of the commanders in the field.[90] Promotion

depended not only on an officer's demonstrated potential for service at a higher grade, but also on

the existence of a vacancy at that higher grade.[91] Thus, promotion opportunity varied drastically

from unit to unit and from time to time. Temporary promotions became commonplace during the

war as a means to boost officer structure where official authorization was nonexistent. By the

end of the war, the decentralized management of officer promotions had left an officer corps that

was large, out-of-balance, and wanting for re-alignment and new direction.

In the wake of World War II, military leaders set about to reform the officer management

systems of the armed forces. Few had forgotten the mobilization challenges of 1940 and 1941

and the painful purges that were required to jump-start the American war machine. Senior Army

leaders vowed that the officer corps would never again degenerate into a retirement community

for old, inefficient, and non-combat-ready officers. After the war, General Dwight D. Eisenhower

commented on the poor state of the officer corps during mobilization:

> Many officers in senior command positions in the Army prior to World War II
> had to be replaced by younger men. On the verge of World War II the Army could not
> rely on most of its senior officers to provide a foundation for higher command of the
> expanded army. If you look at General Marshall's difficulties in 1940 and 1941, I
> believe you will find that of the people he could make division commanders, and corps
> commanders . . . there were not over five of them who went through this war. All the rest
> of them had to be replaced and gotten out of the way and younger men had to come along
> and take over the job.[92]

---

[90] Ibid., 89.

[91] Ibid.

[92] Senate Armed Services Committee, *Officer Personnel Act of 1947*, quoted in Vandergriff, 60-61.

Given these painful memories, it is not surprising that postwar adjustments to officer management focused on three major themes: uniformity between the services, promoting the youth and vigor of the officer corps, and developing a capacity for remobilization.[93] The first major change was implemented by the Officer Personnel Act of 1947 (OPA47)—an attempt by Congress and the Executive Branch "to provide a long-range management framework in which the officer corps could be successfully managed and through which the historical problem of unreadiness for war could be avoided."[94] This legislation created an "up-or-out" promotion system, whereby cohorts of officers would either advance through the ranks according to designated career timelines or be forced out of the service upon the first indication of stagnation. Under OPA47, the Army and Navy would maintain a healthy flow of young and capable officers through specified promotion eligibility points, mandatory separation for officers twice passed over for promotion, and compulsory retirement or separation points for each grade.[95]

Although OPA47 was a marked improvement over the pre-war officer promotion system, it had two great shortcomings. First, it was designed for the small, all-regular force that was supposed to emerge from a decade of down-sizing. As such, it featured statutory grade ceilings that would eventually hamper the ability of the military departments to maintain a large and healthy officer corps on a sustained basis.[96] Second, OPA47 failed to standardize promotion management across the services. While the issue of inter-service uniformity was not necessarily a concern for the individual services, the members of Congress saw this as a significant issue to be corrected over time with subsequent legislation.[97]

---

[93] Rostker, 90.

[94] U.S. Congress. House, *Defense Officer Personnel Management Act*, 96th Cong., 2d sess., 1980, H.Rep. 96-1462, 8.

[95] Ibid., 8-9. Under OPA47, mandatory retirement points (if not selected for promotion) were as follows: colonel: 30 years commissioned service; lieutenant colonel: 28 years; majors: 21 years. Mandatory separation points (if not promoted) were as follows: captains: 14 years; first lieutenants: 7 years.

[96] House, 9.

[97] Ibid, 9-11.

Between 1947 and 1980, Congress used a series of ad hoc legislative changes to deal with the challenges of developing and maintaining the Cold War officer corps. Under OPA47, the Army and the Air Force had no restrictions on the use of temporary promotions. The Officer Grade Limitation Act (OGLA) of 1954 regulated this growing practice by setting limits on the number of regular and reserve officers on active duty in the grades O-4 and above.[98] In response to growing concern over the departure of too many officers at the twenty-year mark, OGLA also attempted to set limits on voluntary retirements. However, the military services won repeal of this provision after predicting (incorrectly) that most officers would serve a full thirty years, even without the provision.[99] Through Air Force grade relief legislation (1959, 1961, 1963), Congress adjusted grade ceilings to prevent high forced attrition rates in the top-heavy and maturing service.[100] These piecemeal adjustments to the officer promotion system paved the way for the pillar of the current officer promotion system—the Defense Officer Personnel Management Act (DOPMA) of 1980.

The Defense Officer Personnel Management Act (DOPMA) of 1980

DOPMA was first introduced in the House of Representatives on 30 January 1974. After six years of debate, the bill was finally passed into law in 1980, and it became effective on 15 September 1981. House Report 96-1462 clearly states the purpose of the bill:

> "to revise the laws that govern the management of commissioned-officer active-duty force. The bill would:
> --Establish new statutory limitations on the number of officer who may serve in senior grades below flag and general officer rank;
> --Provide common law for the appointment of regular officers and for the active-duty service of reserve officers;
> --Provide uniform laws for promotion procedures for officers in the separate services;
> --Establish common provisions governing career expectation in the various grades;

---

[98] Ibid., 10.
[99] Rostker, 95-96.
[100] House.

--Establish common mandatory separation and retirement points for regular commissioned officers;
--Increase the amount of separation pay for officers separated involuntarily short of retirement; and
--Provide related authorities to manage the officer force under the revised personnel system.[101]

The report also describes the bill as "one of the final steps in the evolutionary process begun in 1946 to unify officer promotion and management procedures among the services."[102] Thus, the DOPMA of 1980 was not as forward-looking as members of Congress and the Executive Branch claimed. Rather, a large part of its focus was on solving the officer management issues of the Second World War.

DOPMA remains the central pillar of the officer promotion system in all services of the U.S. military. The Act modified Title 10 of the United States Code in several ways. These modifications pertain not only to officer promotions, but also to many aspects of officer management to including accession, retirement, selective continuation, and constructive credit. Although some of these changes fall outside the realm of officer promotion system, almost all of them have at least an indirect impact on officer promotions. The following discussion will address the main provisions of DOPMA.

DOPMA introduced a grade table—a "structure of allowances" that establishes a "ceiling on the number of officers in each of the grades O-4, O-5, and O-6."[103] The purpose of the grade table is to

--Allow the services to meet requirements for officers in the various grades and ages and levels of experience conducive to effective performance;
--Provide career opportunity that will attract and retain the number of high-caliber officers needed; and
--Provide reasonably consistent career opportunity among the services.[104]

---

[101] House, 3.
[102] Ibid, 12.
[103] House, 13.
[104] House, 14.

The provision designates field grade officer strength as a percentage of total officer strength; it is not tied to total military end-strength.[105] Incorporated in the grade table provision is the "sliding-scale principle." This feature ensures that in the event of mobilization or de-mobilization, "the percentage of field-grade officers does not increase or decrease as rapidly as the strength of the officer corps as a whole."[106] Thus, the sliding-scale principle ensures a relatively constant population of field grade officers, regardless of the total size of each of the services. The grade table does not dictate grade limits for the junior officer grades (O-1 through O-3), for general and flag officers, or for specialists such as doctors and dentists. Since its genesis, the DOPMA grade table has been criticized as an arbitrary and inflexible tool for the management of the officer corps—especially in times of growth or reduction.[107] Nonetheless, the grade table bounds the officer promotion system in all services.

DOPMA also delineates the officer career progression model for all services. Figure 6 contains the chart provided in House Report 96-1462 to illustrate the standardized career progression for all officers. For each grade O-1 through O-6, DOPMA specifies promotion opportunity for each grade (in terms of % selected), promotion timing (in terms of years in service and years in grade), and career expectation (retirement or separation guidance in the event of non-selection). The DOPMA career progression model defines the landmarks in the thirty-year career of a "due-course" officer with the only possible variations being below the zone (BZ) or above the zone (AZ) selection at each of the field grades.[108]

---

[105] Rostker, 7-8.

[106] House, 14.

[107] Rostker, 8-10. Rotsker et al present a detailed criticism of the DOPMA grade table in Chapter 2, pages 8-10. They point out that the grade table was the result of a compromise between the Senate who wanted a reduction in the officer corps and the House of Representatives, backed by the Defense Department, who supported status quo. They also state that despite the rhetoric, the grade table is "not linked to the manpower requirements and personnel authorizations process; it represents *legal* goals to be met rather than needs to be accommodated."

[108] House, 4 gives the following definitions: Due-course officer: an officer "who has neither failed of promotion nor been selected for promotion earlier than his contemporaries." Below the Zone: "persons in this zone have acquired a requisite level of experience but less than that required for the

Figure 6: Dimensions and Characteristics of Defense Officer Promotion System[109]

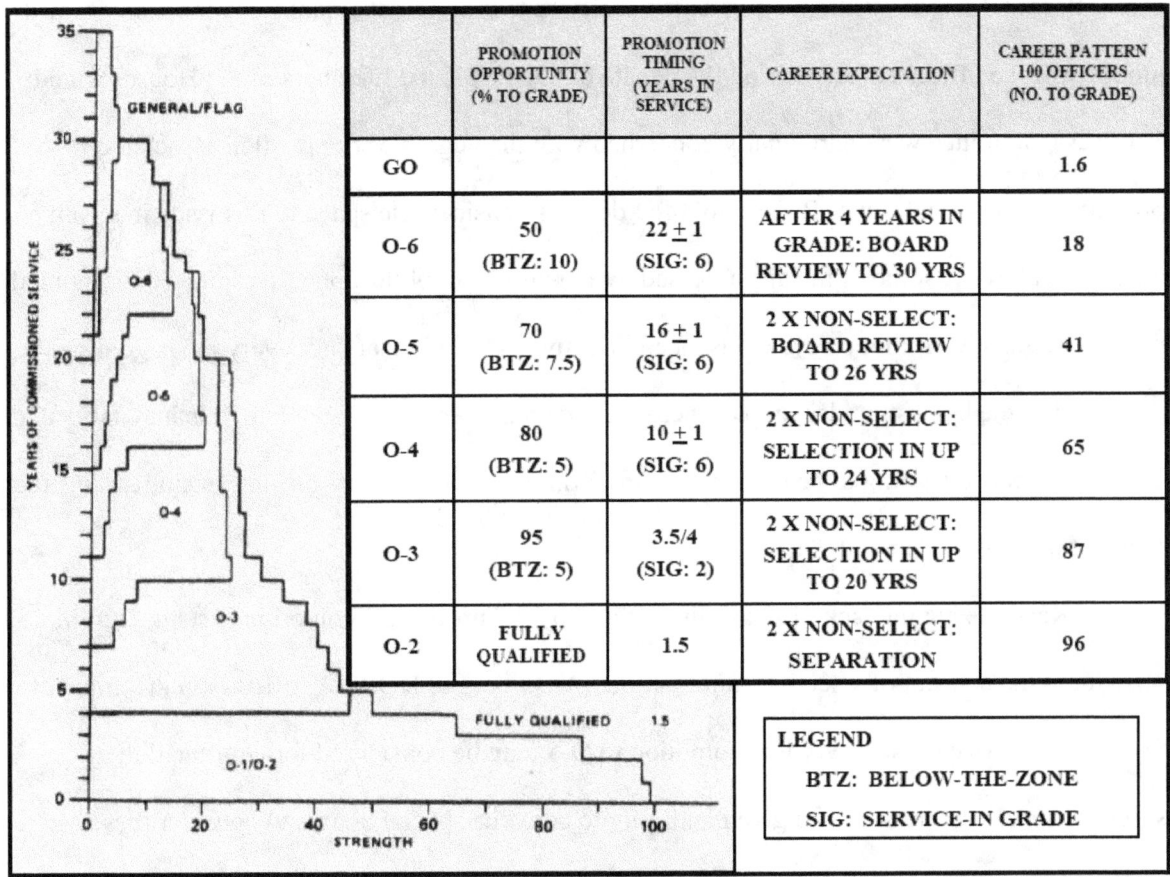

	PROMOTION OPPORTUNITY (% TO GRADE)	PROMOTION TIMING (YEARS IN SERVICE)	CAREER EXPECTATION	CAREER PATTERN 100 OFFICERS (NO. TO GRADE)
GO				1.6
O-6	50 (BTZ: 10)	22 ± 1 (SIG: 6)	AFTER 4 YEARS IN GRADE: BOARD REVIEW TO 30 YRS	18
O-5	70 (BTZ: 7.5)	16 ± 1 (SIG: 6)	2 X NON-SELECT: BOARD REVIEW TO 26 YRS	41
O-4	80 (BTZ: 5)	10 ± 1 (SIG: 6)	2 X NON-SELECT: SELECTION IN UP TO 24 YRS	65
O-3	95 (BTZ: 5)	3.5/4 (SIG: 2)	2 X NON-SELECT: SELECTION IN UP TO 20 YRS	87
O-2	FULLY QUALIFIED	1.5	2 X NON-SELECT: SEPARATION	96

LEGEND
BTZ: BELOW-THE-ZONE
SIG: SERVICE-IN GRADE

The combination of the grade table and the career progression model (with its specified retirement and separation rules) forms the central feature of DOPMA—the up-or-out promotion system. The House Report reminds the reader that there "is nothing new about this concept [of up-or-out]. It has been in effect for nearly 35 years and on the whole has served the country well. The system has given the armed forces what they never before had in peacetime—a youthful, vigorous, *fully* combat-ready officer corps."[110] Under the up-or-out system, officers are expected to progress through their career in designated cohorts, competing for promotion at specified

---

primary zone." Above the Zone (AZ): "persons in this zone have more than the requisite level of experience for promotion and have failed selection by at least one previous selection board."

[109] Adapted from House, 18.

[110] House, 19.

eligibility points. Officers who twice fail promotion are separated or retired. Through specified career flow and forced attrition, up-or-out is designed to maintain the quality, youth, and upward mobility of the officer corps. During the debate on DOPMA, the members of the House Armed Services Committee were particularly concerned with the negative stigma often associated with promotion pass-over. House Report 96-1462 devotes considerable space to this issue in a vain attempt to alleviate some of the angst caused by the up-or-out philosophy. Despite Congressional reminders that the promotion system is "a competitive system," that "not everyone is going to be promoted to the highest grades, in part, because not all are required," and that "it is inevitable that capable officers are going to be passed over from time to time," the up–or-out system remains the focus of much criticism and debate.[111]

Recognizing the lack of flexibility offered by the up-or-out promotion system, DOPMA introduces the concept of selective continuation. According to DOPMA, officers in the grade of O-4 who are twice passed-over for promotion to O-5 may be considered for continuation of service. Service Secretaries are given authority to convene special boards to consider these officers for continuation. Officers selected by the board are permitted to continue service in the current grade until the normal twenty-year mandatory separation point. According to DOPMA, these officers "would not be again subjected to board action."[112] Officers not selected for continuation would be separated from service under normal separation procedures (including separation pay if not eligible for retirement). Contrary to current trends towards extensive offerings of selective continuation, the drafters of DOPMA intended for the provision "to be used sparingly" and primarily "as a means of reducing the numbers in senior grades when necessary, such as during a reduction in force."[113]

---

[111] House, 19.
[112] House, 27.
[113] House, 27.

A critical focus of DOPMA is the standardization of promotion procedures across all services. According to the law, each service must establish a single "active duty list [that] would be used to determine eligibility for promotion and to provide for a proper timing of the promotion system."[114] This centrally-managed list is the basis for all determinations related to officer promotions to include determination of eligibility zones, grade limits, and promotion selection or failure based on specified promotion opportunity. Interestingly, the Army, Navy, and Air Force have each developed unique ways to manage this active duty list, and each method results in distinct nuances in officer promotion timing and opportunity within the separate services.[115]

Other Pillars of the Officer Promotion System

DOPMA is the central pillar of the officer promotion system. There are, however, other elements of the system that should be mentioned briefly.

Congress issues routine guidance on officer promotions through National Defense Authorization Acts. These laws are generally focused on temporary adjustments to the total force end strength and as such, may have a temporary impact on the DOPMA grade table. Regardless, these legislative measures continue to support the assumptions and implementation principles of DOPMA.

The Defense Department issues formal instructions to the service Secretaries to guide their implementation of the promotion system. Department of Defense Instruction (DODI) 1320.13, published 21 June, 1996, outlines reporting guidance and procedures for commissioned officer promotions within all services. This directive establishes the Commissioned Officer Promotion Report (COPR) and assigns responsibility for preparing and rendering this report

---

[114] House, 24.

[115] Rostker, 15-16. The authors detail the differences in ADL management procedures within the separate services and the impact of these procedures on promotion opportunity and timing.

within each of the Service Departments.[116] Department of Defense Instruction 1320.14,

published September 24, 1996, details the procedures for the Commissioned Officer Promotion

Program. This instruction assigns responsibilities for implementation of the program and it

dictates procedure for the conduct of promotion selection boards.[117] Both of these formal

Defense Department Instructions operate well within the dictates of DOPMA and Title 10 USC.

The Department of the Army further defines the officer promotion system for Army

officers through regulations, pamphlets, and policies. *Army Regulation 600-8-3, Officer*

Promotions assigns responsibilities, defines principles and standards, and outlines procedures for

the management of promotion for commissioned officers in the Army.[118] *Department of the*

Army Pamphlet 600-3, Commissioned Officer Development and Career Management, further

defines the officer promotion system by explaining its link with Officer Personnel Management

System 3 (OPMS 3). This pamphlet also explains the key provisions of DOPMA to include time-

in-service and time-in-grade requirements, tenure rules, and career opportunity for each officer

grade.[119] Fine-tuning of the officer promotion system is accomplished through policy letters from

the Army Deputy Chief of Staff for Personnel (G-1) and from Human Resources Command.

Again, these documents instruct the Army on how it will implement the promotion system as

specified by law; they offer no major deviations from the provisions of DOPMA.

Thus, the essence of the Army officer promotion system resides in Title 10, USC as

altered by DOPMA. While Army regulations, policies, and directives delineate the specifics of

implementation, the primary principles of officer promotions are strictly bounded by law.

---

[116] U.S. Department of Defense, *Department of Defense Instruction Number 1320.13: Commissioned Officer Promotion Reports (COPRs) and Procedures* (Washington, D.C.: 21 June, 1996).

[117] U.S. Department of Defense, *Department of Defense Instruction Number 1320.14: Commissioned Officer Promotion Program Procedures* (Washington, D.C.: 24 September, 1996).

[118] U.S. Department of the Army, *AR 600-8-29, Officer Promotion* (Washington, D.C.: 2004).

[119] *DA PAM 600-3*, 20-22.

Assumptions and Principles of the Officer Promotion System

The framers of DOPMA did not explicitly list their assumptions. Likewise, Title 10 USC fails to specify the underlying assumptions of the officer promotion system. Nonetheless, a careful analysis of the provisions of the system makes one fact clear: the officer promotion system is laden with tacit assumptions that translate into strict implementation principles. Figure 7 lists these assumptions and illustrates their link with implementation principles. Many of the assumptions and principles listed have been scrutinized and criticized in recent years as being outdated, invalid, or irrelevant to today's Army and Defense Department. Moreover, several of these assumptions conflict directly with Army efforts to change the manning paradigm. The following discussion will review these assumptions, assess their current validity, and determine their congruence with the ongoing UFS initiative.

Figure 7: Assumptions and Principles of the Officer Promotion System and their Conflicts with UFS

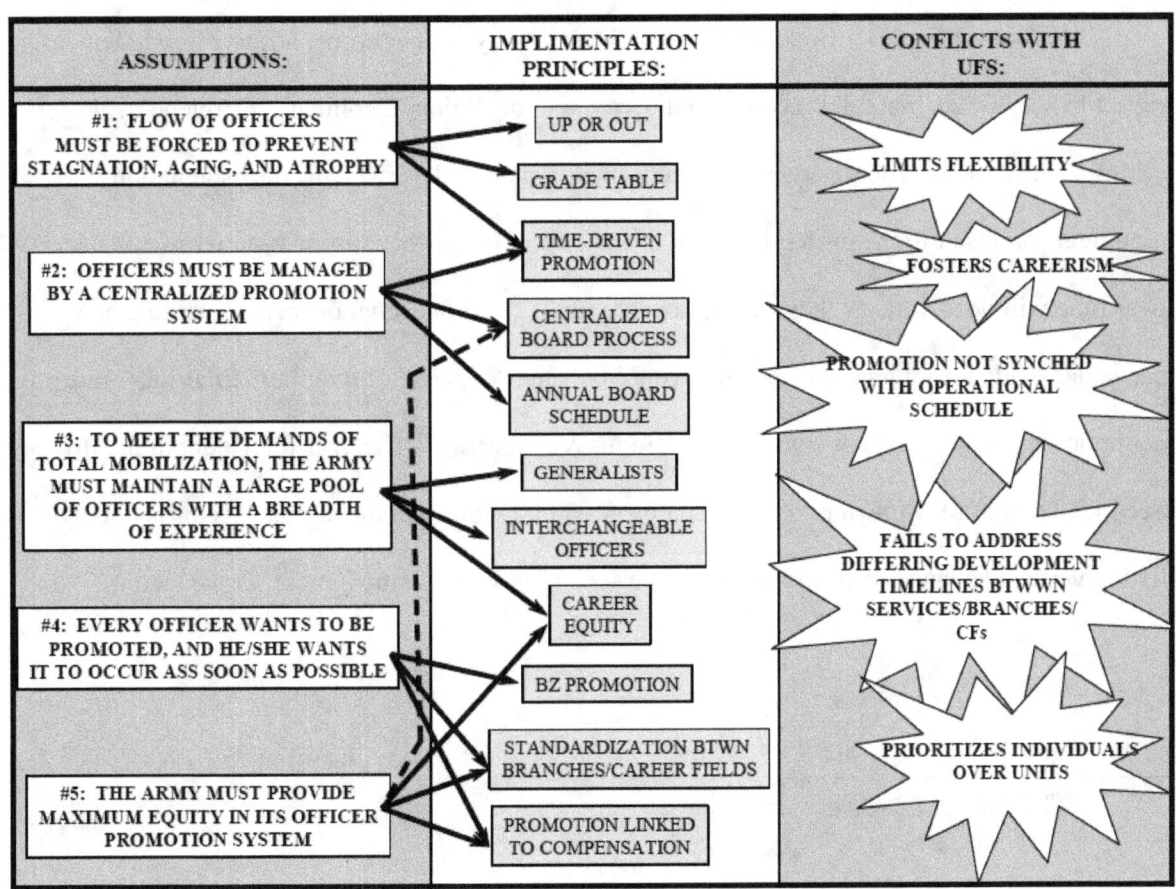

Assumption #1: Flow of Officers must be forced to prevent stagnation, aging, and atrophy.

As discussed at the beginning of this chapter, the history of the officer corps is one of military unreadiness at the outset of war. This lack of readiness was the product of a promotion system based on seniority and lacking effective forced attrition systems. Given the Army's poor track record in this regard, it is no surprise that this first assumption is such a driving factor in the current management of officers. Assumption #1 translates directly into one of the fundamental implementation principles of the officer promotion system: the principle of "up-or-out." The up-or-out philosophy translates directly into other key elements of the system, including the grade table (with its aggressive career timelines and graduated career expectation) and forced attrition policies.

Is Assumption #1 still valid today? Will the Army officer corps, left to its own devices, repeat history by stagnating, breeding mediocrity, and declining in combat effectiveness? Many critics of the current officer personnel system think not. Vandergriff calls the "stagnation argument" an insult to the professionalism of the officer corps "because it assumes that officers over time will do as little as they can get away with."[120] Professional officers remaining at a particular grade for long periods of time would become "experts" in their particular job—rare commodities in an up-or-out environment. In his recent essay, "The War for Talent in the Private Sector," Thomas M. Strawn points out that professional vitality in the civilian sector is not always tied to vertical advancement; rather, it is often fostered by lateral movement, broadened

---

[120] Vandergriff, 245.

48

experiences, increased opportunities for learning.[121] Obviously, slowing the rate of promotion

will lead to an older officer corps. However, this will not necessarily lead to a drop in combat

effectiveness. Combat operations remain a young man's business, but improved health and

fitness in society as a whole and the Army in general may change the age threshold for combat

leaders. Additionally, while technology is certainly not a panacea, it may reduce physical

demands thereby enabling older officers to lead companies, battalions, and brigades in combat.

Perhaps blanket policies aimed at maintaining a young officer corps should be replaced by a

system to evaluate the individual fitness of an officer for continued service in his particular

specialty. Such a system would be in line with recent Congressional and Defense Department

guidance to use individual standards of health and fitness to determine eligibility for continued

service.[122] Nonetheless, history underscores the need for some form of managed attrition in the

officer corps, and this requirement will likely continue into the future.

Assumption #1 will be a key contributor to officer friction points under UFS. The

traditional emphasis on the youth and vigor of the officer corps has lead to aggressive and

inflexible career timelines that do not support efforts towards unit cohesion. According to

Vandergriff, the most "detrimental impact of the up-or-out promotion system is that it undercuts

trust among officers by creating constant promotion anxiety. . . ."[123]. As discussed in Chapter 2,

the rapid advancement through the lieutenant ranks creates significant friction in brigade combat

teams under the Lifecycle Management model. Likewise, the short window for majors to

complete schooling and branch qualification brings officer career advancement in direct conflict

with quest for unit cohesion under UFS.

---

[121] Thomas M. Strawn, "The War for Talent in the Private Sector," in *Filling the Ranks: Transforming the U.S. Military Personnel System*, ed. Cindy Williams, 69-91 (Cambridge: MIT Press, 2004), 89.

[122] Harry J. Thie et al, "Future Career Management Systems for U.S. Military Officers" (Santa Monica: RAND Corporation, 1994), 198.

[123] Vandergriff, 243.

The concern for the health and vitality of the officer remains a legitimate one for the contemporary Army. However, the assumption that officer flow must be "forced" is no longer valid. Officer flow in today's Army should be "monitored" and "managed." The methods used to prevent stagnation and ensure combat readiness should be made more flexible. A healthy and committed officer corps can enjoy more flexibility in its officer promotion system without danger of force-wide atrophy.

Assumption #2: Officers must be managed by a centralized promotion system.

DOPMA was the capstone of a long trend toward centralization and standardization in officer management across the services. This trend began in the early 1900's and for most, it was viewed as the key to successful management of the colossal military machines of World War I and World War II.[124] As American Corporations of the 1950's hailed the benefits of centralization, the Army followed suit.[125] By the 1980's, every major personnel process— including senior NCO and officer promotions and command selection—was managed at Department of the Army level.[126] The assumed need for centralization has been hard-wired into every facet of personnel management in the Army. Many assume there is no other option for effective, efficient, and equitable management of a large organization like the Army.

A look at human resource management in today's corporate world highlights a new trend toward decentralization. A 1994 study by the National Defense Research Institute suggests that private sector companies faced with the prospects of downsizing are seeking greater flexibility by leaving matters of personnel management to the lower levels of the business organization. According to the study, "subordinate business units have more control over precise policies on

---

[124] John C. F. Tillson, "Reducing the Impact of Tempo" (Alexandria: Institute for Defense Analyses, 1999) http://www.d-n-i.net/fcs/tillson_tempo.pdf. (accessed September 2, 2004), S-4
[125] Ibid., S-5.
[126] Ibid.

hiring, advancing, developing, and position controls."[127] In a 1999 study, John C.F. Tillson of the

Institute for Defense Analyses made the following observation:

> American corporations shifted away from centralized personnel management
> systems years ago. The 8th Quadrennial Review of Military Compensation concluded
> that such a shift would be appropriate for the military departments as well . . . The
> Military Services should examine whether a modern, decentralized personnel system
> would better meet the needs of individuals and units.[128]

Certainly, the mission of private sector companies differs greatly from that of the Army.

However, as both of these Defense Department-sponsored studies highlight, the examples of

these other organization are cause enough for reevaluation of the assumed requirement for

centralization.

Considered in isolation, the centralized nature of the current officer promotion system

does not hinder the implementation of UFS. The fact that promotion boards and associated

processes are centralized at Department level removes a heavy administrative burden from the

commanders and staffs in the brigade combat teams. However, when centralized management is

combined with the effects of aggressive career timelines, strict branch qualification requirements,

and forced attrition policies, the result is a significant reduction in flexibility. Without flexibility

in officer management, the Army cannot make the leap to unit manning.

Assumption #3: To meet the demands of full mobilization, the Army must maintain a large pool of officers with a breadth of experience.

Assumption #3 is product of American mobilization experiences in World War I and

World War II. Likewise, it is a relic of the Cold War environment in which the national security

strategy called for a huge pool of officers to serve as the cadre for total mobilization against a

---

[127] Thie, 125.
[128] Ibid.

Soviet threat.[129] To create and maintain this cadre, the services designed personnel systems that rapidly promoted officers through the junior grades, maximizing breadth over depth of experience. The up-or-out philosophy was essential for maintaining a healthy surplus of mid-level leaders while also eliminating those that were too old for service in a long war against the Soviets.[130]

The focus on mobilization drives the Army towards three implementation principles that pervade many areas of officer management.   The first of these principles is "every officer a generalist." This concept has its origins with General George C. Marshall, whose mobilization vision for the Army has shaped personnel policies for the last fifty years. According to this concept, officers are moved through numerous assignments and duties throughout their career in order to maximize their command and staff experiences. In the event of mobilization, the varied experiences of these officers will prepare them to "lead millions of soldiers in new, larger formations."[131] Closely related to the generalist principle is the principle of "interchangeability."[132] To ease the management burden in the event of mobilization, officers must have a certain degree of interchangeability. Such "assembly-line" interchangeability drives the officer management systems towards inflexible personnel management policies; to create interchangeable officers, career development tracks and promotion timelines must be highly standardized and closely managed. With the introduction of OPMS 3, this principle was eliminated for about 30% of mid-level Army officers, but for the majority of the force, it remains in tact. Over time, these first two principles have created a third: the principle of career equity. The American traditions of egalitarianism and fairness still dominate Army personnel systems. The challenge of moving a surplus of officers through numerous assignments according to

---

[129] Tillson.
[130] Ibid.
[131] Vandergriff, 80-81.
[132] Tillson, 20.

standardized career templates makes true career equity elusive. However, the Army personnel system remains anchored to the principle of equity.

Many argue that the days of total mobilization are gone. Tillson writes, "The National Security Strategy no longer contemplates total mobilization or a long war. Instead, the plan calls for full mobilization of existing active and reserve forces."[133] Tillson also recommends that the services "eliminate the vestiges of total mobilization and long war planning that are no longer needed to meet the current National Security Strategy."[134] In her 2004 book, *Filling the Ranks: Transforming the U.S. Military Personnel System*, Dr. Cindy Williams criticizes service personnel systems that are bound by "mobilization-motivated rules" and thus, are ill-equipped to recruit, develop, promote, or retain the officers and soldiers required to meet the demands of the post-9/11 world.[135] The realities of the current strategic environment make Assumption #3 invalid.

The continued focus on mobilization indirectly affects UFS. The mobilization mindset translates directly into the up-or-out promotion philosophy and the inflexible grade table management system. Each of these creates careerist tendencies and a "ticket-punching" mindset among officers that is detrimental to efforts at unit cohesion. By declaring the mobilization assumption invalid and by aligning promotion and personnel policies with the new strategic realities, the Army may gain the flexibility required for UFS.

Assumption #4: Every officer wants to be promoted, and he/she wants it to occur as soon as possible.

Promotion in the Army brings with it several positive features for the individual officer. Among these are increased pay and compensation, increased status, and improved housing.

---

[133] Ibid., S-5.
[134] Ibid.

Given these benefits, it is easy to assume that an officer will always desire promotion and that the sooner it comes, the better. However, this may not always be true. Shortly after an officer is selected for advancement, he is hit with the realization that there is, indeed, a "down-side" to promotion. Before pin-on ever occurs, the typical officer will face prospects of forced duty changes (often requiring a Permanent Change of Station), added responsibility, and new career "gates" with their associated time pressures. Perhaps one cannot assume that promotion is always welcomed by every officer at all times.

Several authors have investigated the essence of Assumption #4 and found its validity questionable at best. In a 2000 U.S. Army War College Research Project, Jeffrey S. White applied the business world concept of "Voluntary Simplicity" to the Army:

> The business world increasingly sees workers who are refusing to allow a fast track career put their personal lives in a position of secondary importance. These employees are *voluntarily simplifying* [emphasis added] their personal lives by choosing to step off the treadmill leading to promotion and advancement. Specifically, this may mean refusing to relocate or turning down a promotion that may require longer hours or additional responsibilities. Putting family first and pursuing a better quality of life has become increasingly more important to many people than inching up the corporate ladder. . . .
>
> Like the business world, the United States Army increasingly finds that not all of its officers are driven to be a success at the higher echelons of command and staff. Many officers have jobs they find inherently satisfying and would prefer to continue within that scope regardless of its effects on their potential in front of the next selection board. Just as business recognizes the principle of *Voluntary Simplification* [emphasis added] can enhance the organization, so must the Army.[136]

Thomas Strawn expresses the same idea in his 2004 essay, stating, "there are individuals who do not want to move up, but prefer to be the best at whatever they now do, performing at a very high level."[137] Sadly, the aggressive career timelines of DOPMA and the up-or-out philosophy do not allow the luxury of "Voluntary Simplification."

---

[135] Cindy Williams, ed. *Filling the Ranks: Transforming the U.S. Military Personnel System* (Cambridge: MIT Press, 2004), 303-331.

[136] Jeffrey S. White, "Getting to the Business of Officer Personnel Management" (Strategy Research Project, U.S. Army War College, 2000) 5.

[137] Strawn.

If one assumes that officers always desire rapid promotion, then implementation principles like up-or-out, grade table management, and below zone selection are easily justified by lawmakers and policymakers. Unfortunately, each of these practices conflicts directly with any effort to prioritize unit cohesion over individual career progression. The current officer promotion system teaches officers to value increased rank, responsibility, and compensation over job proficiency and unit cohesion. Undoubtedly, officers do concern themselves with issues like individual status, pay, and benefits. Elizabeth A. Stanley-Mitchell argues that with the bureaucratization of the military through rigid career paths and inflexible promotion policies, the military professional has become increasingly focused on tangible compensation.[138] Army systems and policies tend to degrade the intangible rewards of professional development, increased proficiency, and unit performance, yet these same intangibles are, in fact, critically important to individual officers. Tillson concludes that service members demand both "security *and* satisfaction."[139] The former meets the demands of Maslow's hierarchy of needs; the latter meets the individual's desires for fulfillment through self-actualization.[140]

A promotion system designed to support the implementation of UFS must provide officers with reasonable security and job satisfaction. One cannot assume that an officers always wants to be promoted, nor can one assume that rapid advancement improves officer morale. Instead, the promotion system must provide adequate tangible rewards, while giving officers the flexibility to achieve the intangible rewards that come with building cohesive, combat-effective teams.

---

[138] Elizabeth A. Stanley-Mitchell, "The Military Profession and Intangible Rewards for Service," in *Filling the Ranks: Transforming the U.S. Military Personnel System,* ed. Cindy Williams, 93-118 (Cambridge: MIT Press, 2004) 113.

[139] Tillson, 32.

[140] Ibid.

Assumption #5: The Army must provide maximum equity in its officer promotion system.

This assumption is tied very closely to the generalist principle. In the aftermath of World War II, personnel managers in the Army gave birth to the concept of "career equity." Not only was this practice of equity tied to fundamental American ideals of fairness and opportunity, it was also critical to Marhsall's concept that every officer must be a general manager with basic experience in a variety of areas.[141] Equity has become fundamental to all aspects of personnel management in the Army. This is especially so in the area of officer promotions. *Department of the Army Pamphlet 600-3* clearly expresses the equity assumption by stating that the officer promotion system "must be administered fairly and equitably; to do otherwise would jeopardize the effectiveness of the officer corps."[142]

From the equity assumption spring three key implementation principles. First among these is the principle of standardization—that is, the requirement for identical promotion timing, procedures, and opportunity across most branches and career fields. Despite the fact that development timelines and requirements may differ between individual officer specialties, the focus on equity forces maximum standardization. The second principle is that of centralized consideration. Under the centralized promotion system, promotion consideration is taken out of the hands of an officer's chain of command and put into the hands of a disinterested, semi-anonymous, and supposedly unbiased centralized promotion board. This procedure allows Army-level oversight into the promotion selection process, allegedly removing local bias and preventing cronyism. Finally, the equity assumption has produced officer grade and pay scales that are almost inextricably linked. In fact, it is fair to state that the link between rank and pay are a fundamental part of Army culture. Perhaps no greater sense of equity is provided for officers

---

[141] Vandergriff, 82-83.

than the knowledge that a Captain of Infantry with eight years time in service is paid the same as a Captain of Finance with the same time in service. While it is commonly understood and accepted that officers serving as pilots, doctors, and lawyers are paid more for their specialized (and highly marketable) expertise, imagine the impact of a complete de-linking of promotion and pay. Under the weight of a diversified officer pay scale, the current concept of equity and its associated principles would crumble.

Each of these equity-based implementation principles adds friction to the UFS model. Standardization of the promotion system across branches and career fields limits the flexibility of Army leaders to manage an officer corps with diverse development requirements. A combat arms officer under Lifecycle Management may require one career timeline, while a logistics officer at Echelons Above Corps (EAC) may require another. The principle of standardization and the linkage between promotion and pay creates a formidable barrier that prevents flexible and diversified management. The centralized promotion board fosters careerism among officer. Instead of rewarding unit performance, encouraging selfless service, and fostering teamwork— the things that are so critical to the success of any unit manning system—the centralized board process focuses officers on the Officer Evaluation Reports (OERs), official photos, and Officer Record Briefs. For UFS to succeed, the Army must re-define equity.

Time to Review Assumptions?

The Army is attempting to make the bold shift to a unit-centric manning system. This significant change will require maximum flexibility in officer management. Unfortunately, the current officer promotion system lacks such pliancy. The primary cause is the fact that it is based on fifty-year-old assumptions that are not valid for today's Army. Figure 8 summarizes this disconnect between old assumptions and reality.

---

[142] DA PAM 600-3, 20.

Figure 8: Old Assumptions and New Reality[143]

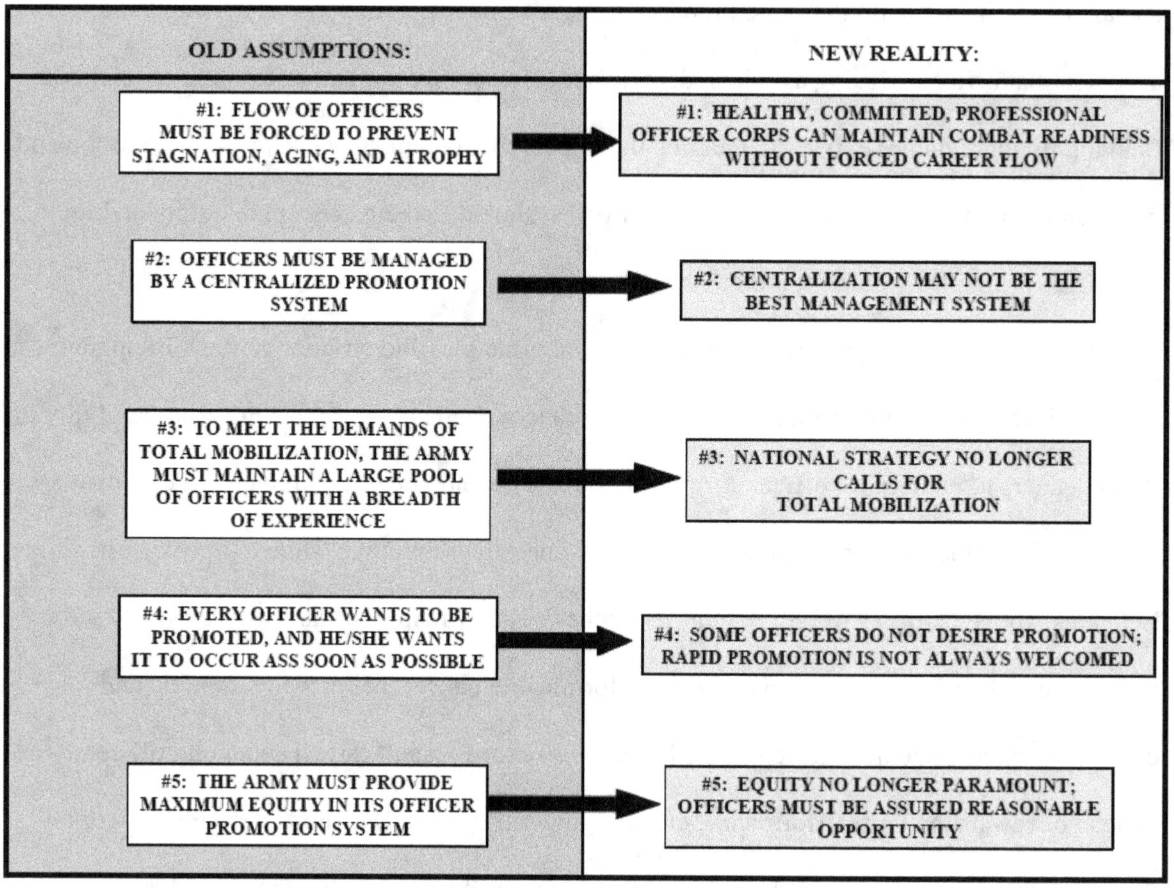

OLD ASSUMPTIONS:	NEW REALITY:
#1: FLOW OF OFFICERS MUST BE FORCED TO PREVENT STAGNATION, AGING, AND ATROPHY	**#1: HEALTHY, COMMITTED, PROFESSIONAL OFFICER CORPS CAN MAINTAIN COMBAT READINESS WITHOUT FORCED CAREER FLOW**
#2: OFFICERS MUST BE MANAGED BY A CENTRALIZED PROMOTION SYSTEM	**#2: CENTRALIZATION MAY NOT BE THE BEST MANAGEMENT SYSTEM**
#3: TO MEET THE DEMANDS OF TOTAL MOBILIZATION, THE ARMY MUST MAINTAIN A LARGE POOL OF OFFICERS WITH A BREADTH OF EXPERIENCE	**#3: NATIONAL STRATEGY NO LONGER CALLS FOR TOTAL MOBILIZATION**
#4: EVERY OFFICER WANTS TO BE PROMOTED, AND HE/SHE WANTS IT TO OCCUR ASS SOON AS POSSIBLE	**#4: SOME OFFICERS DO NOT DESIRE PROMOTION; RAPID PROMOTION IS NOT ALWAYS WELCOMED**
#5: THE ARMY MUST PROVIDE MAXIMUM EQUITY IN ITS OFFICER PROMOTION SYSTEM	**#5: EQUITY NO LONGER PARAMOUNT; OFFICERS MUST BE ASSURED REASONABLE OPPORTUNITY**

Assumptions shape organizational policies. Policies define organizational values. Values determine organizational culture.[144] The tacit assumptions of the officer promotion system espouse the values of individual advancement, career mobility, and equity. Over time, these values have created an officer culture that will be a significant impediment to any attempt at changing the manning paradigm.

The Army must review the underlying assumptions of the officer promotion system. Many of the old assumptions are common across the Defense Department, and all are hard-wired into current law and policy. Thus, any change to these foundations of officer management will be

---

[143] Adapted from Tillson, 46.

difficult, but not impossible. When asked to list assumptions for the re-design of OPMS3, a recent Council of Colonels wrote, "Current laws can be changed."[145] Certainly, this is a positive sign that Army leadership is ready to make difficult systemic changes to meet the demands of the future.

CHAPTER FOUR: OPTIONS FOR CHANGE

In the last several years, the Army personnel system has been the target of significant criticism. Though usually not in the direct line of fire, the officer promotion system gets a fair amount of residual attention. The few reviews aimed directly at officer promotions focus primarily on fiscal issues, and for solutions, these authors turn to private sector organizations to find better and more efficient ways of managing promotions. While these suggestions may bring efficiency to an outdated system, few of their solutions focus specifically on increasing unit cohesion and building effective combat teams.

The purpose of this chapter is to present possible changes to the officer promotion system that will support the implementation and sustainment of UFS. Three options will be presented. The basic aspects of each option will be discussed, and the advantages and disadvantages for each will be listed. This chapter will also discuss the changes to other Army systems that must occur in conjunction with recommended changes to promotions. Finally, this discussion will briefly compare the options and make recommendations on the way ahead.

---

[144] William F. Bell, "The Impact of Policies on Organizational Values and Culture." http://usafa.af.mil/jscope/JSCOPE99/Bell99 html (accessed November 12, 2004).

[145] U.S. Army Human Resources Command, "OPMS3 Council of Colonels 31 Aug – 2 Sep 04," Slide presentation, https://www.perscom.army mil/opfamdd/LDD3 Hotwash.pps (accessed November 12, 2004) slide 25.

Option #1: Replace Up-or-Out with Up-or-Stay

Many authors have proposed an up-or-stay promotion system as a great solution for officer promotion in the Army. The essence of up-or-stay is that it allows "individuals to enjoy full careers even if they do not advance beyond certain positions or levels."[146] The Defense Manpower Commission (DMC) of 1979 recommended that the up-or-out system apply for officers until their tenth year of service. At that point, the officers would fall under an up-or-stay system, that is, their continued service would not be contingent upon promotion.[147] The 1979 Faith/Ross study recommend a similar up-or-stay concept, although its solution focused heavily on the decentralization of promotions, giving increased promotion authority to regimental commanders.[148] Contemporary authors like Vandergriff and Rostker recommend an up-or-stay system that begins with competitive selection into a "career force" after several years of commissioned service. Vandergriff proposes entry into career status upon selection for captain, contingent upon competitive examinations and a semi-centralized selection process.[149] According to Rostker's vision, mid-level officers would face a highly competitive centralized selection process in which only thirty percent would be chosen for the career force. The point of entry into the career force would depend upon the needs of the individual branches and career specialties.[150] According to both models, officers selected as "career officers" would enjoy a

---

[146] Peter Schirmer et al, "New Paths to Success: Determining Career Alternatives for Field-Grade Officers" (Santa Monica: RAND Corporation, 2004) http://www.rand.org/publications/MG/MG117.html. (accessed September 2, 2004), 2-3.

[147] Vandergriff, 111.

[148] Vandergriff, 123-125. As explained by Vandergriff, the Faith/Ross study was commissioned in 1979 by the TRADOC Commander, GEN Don Starry. He asked two allied officers, LTC P.W. Faith of the British Army and LTC R.I. Ross of Canada to study the regimental systems of their own countries and make recommendations about how such regimental systems could be incorporated in the U.S. Army. Naturally, each of their recommendations, including their recommendation for an up-or-stay promotion system, had a clear regimental focus.

[149] Vandergriff, 230.

[150] Bernard Rostker, "Changing the Officer Personnel System," in *Filling the Ranks: Transforming the U.S. Military Personnel System,* ed. Cindy Williams, 146-166 (Cambridge: MIT Press, 2004), 160.

guarantee of continued service until retirement. Of course, forced separation would still be possible due to misconduct, ineptitude, or drawdown.

There are many arguments in favor of an up-or-stay promotion philosophy. At the macro level, up-or-stay would result in lower personnel turnover, which in turn would lead to greater career stability, a more experienced officer corps, and reduced accessions and training costs.[151] Up-or-stay would reduce the angst of the officer corps over long-term job security. Perhaps this small relief in angst would reduce the levels of careerism and unhealthy competition between officers that is so detrimental to cohesion and team building. Because of the advantages of such a system, most foreign militaries use an up-or-stay system for promotion of officers above the grade of O-4.[152]

Even an optimal up-or-stay system would contribute only indirectly to the success of UFS. Up-or-stay would relieve careerist pressure for mid-level officers once they are selected for career status. To some degree, this relief in pressure would free officers to worry less about personal job security and more about building effective teams. However, up-or-stay may relieve pressure for one group while increasing angst for another. The point of selection into the career force would determine where this pressure relief would be felt and more importantly, where careerist pressures would increase. If Captain were the entry point into tenure status, then lieutenants would experience increased career pressures and increased competition for the limited spaces for career officers. If Major were the entry point, then captains would experience the same level of stress and angst experienced before 2004 with the highly competitive Command and Staff College (CSC) selection process.[153] Thus, while up-or-stay would relieve some careerist

---

[151] Schirmer, 3.

[152] Thie, 115.

[153] Before the introduction of "Universal Intermediate Level Education (ILE)" in 2004, captains and junior majors competed for resident attendance at a Command and Staff College. At its most competitive, this process saw only 20% of a given cohort selected for resident schooling during its first year of eligibility and 30% of that same original cohort selected for second year attendance.

pressures for a select group of mid-level officers, it would do little to help officers in brigade combat teams. At best, up-or-stay would leave careerist dynamics largely unaffected within these brigades. At worst, up-or-stay could add additional friction to brigade-level officer management.

Up-or-stay would require at least three other changes to Army systems. First, the pay tables would have to be adjusted to ensure a proper correlation between officer expertise (vice officer rank) and compensation. Second, the retirement system would also need to be changed to accommodate twenty-year captains or thirty-year majors. Finally, force managers would have to conduct a complete audit of Army structure to re-align it with the realities of the new officer demographics that would be created by an up-or-stay system. Each of these changes would have significant fiscal implications that would have to be studied carefully by budgetary experts.

In sum, the adoption of an up-or-stay system should be seen as a macro-level enhancement that would provide overarching top cover for the UFS initiative. It would do little to eliminate the friction of officer management within brigade combat teams. Rather, up-or-stay would mitigate the long-term effects of prioritizing unit cohesion over individual career advancement.

Option #2: Lengthen Career Timelines

The friction points described in Chapter 2 highlight the fact that UFS is severely hamstrung by the time-driven nature of the current officer promotion system. One way to relieve the time pressure is to slow promotion and lengthen the career timeline for officers. Such a change would leave officers in each grade for longer periods of time, and it would create wider windows of opportunity for selection to the next grade.

To support UFS, officer career timelines should be synchronized with the three-year lifecycles that will be created by UFS. According to the friction point analysis in Chapter 2, most lieutenants and captains under Lifecycle Management cannot meet all professional development requirements in one three-year lifecycle. Thus, an improved promotion system should give them two three-year lifecycles in which to serve in they key developmental positions and additional time to attend important military schools. To provide additional flexibility for individual officers, the zones of consideration could be widened from two years to three years. The system would retain its up-or-out philosophy yet reduce the time pressure by providing an additional opportunity to compete for promotion. Figure 9 illustrates the proposed career timeline.

Figure 9: Proposed and Current Officer Promotion Timelines

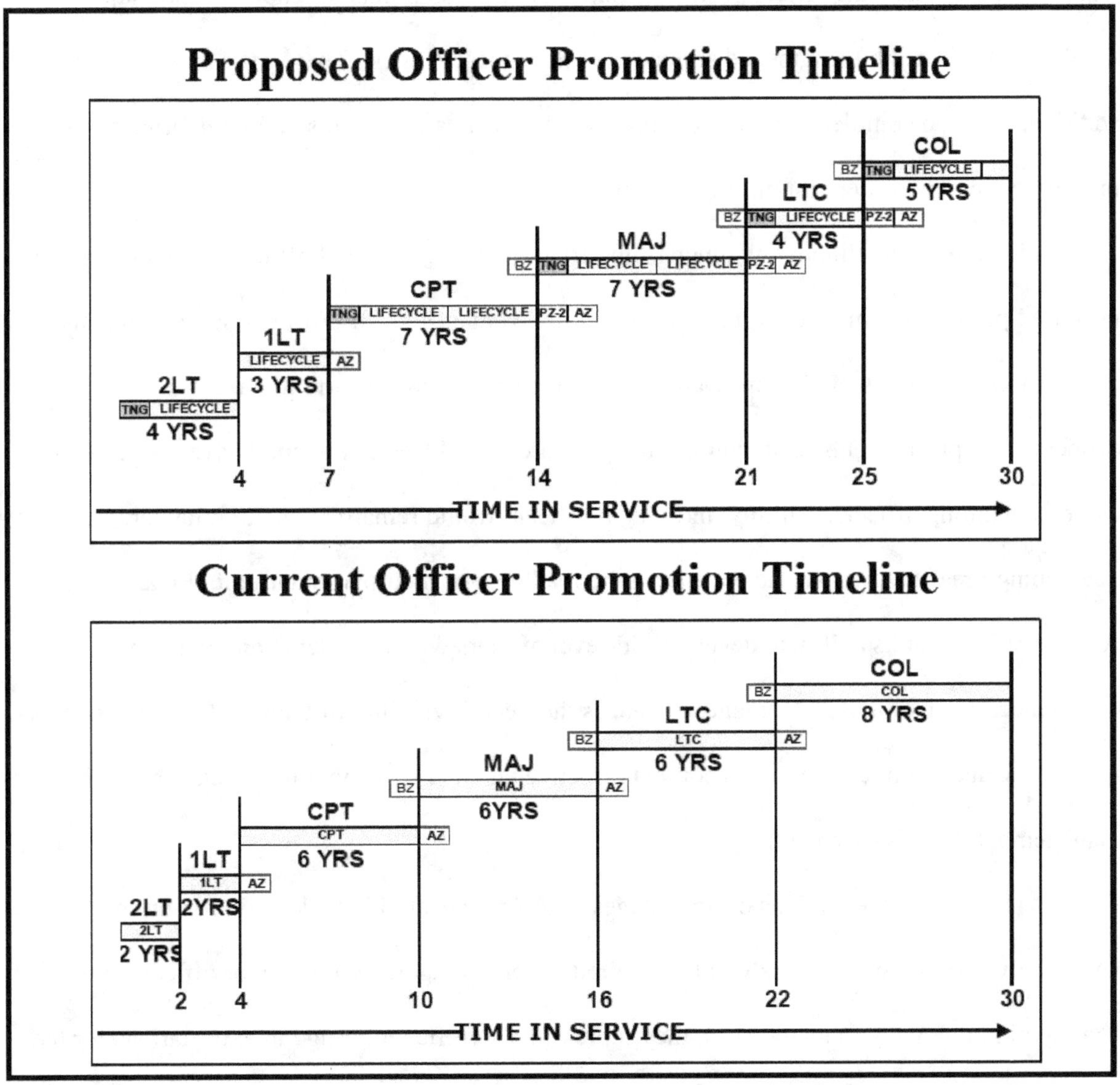

The lengthened career timelines would virtually eliminate many of the friction points described in Chapter 2. Second lieutenants would have four years to complete Initial Entry

Training and then serve in a brigade combat team. At the end of the four years, they would be eligible for promotion to first lieutenant, and they could move to a new brigade combat team during its "Reset" phase. As explained in Chapter 2, the current system presents the commanders within Lifecycle units a dilemma in terms of how to fill critical positions traditionally held by experienced first lieutenants. The proposed system would eliminate this friction point by giving commanders a cohort of first lieutenants to fill the critical executive officer, specialty platoon leader, and assistant staff officer positions. Likewise, friction points for captains and majors would be eliminated by lengthened service at each of these grades. These officers would have additional time to complete their critical branch-qualifying assignments before entering the primary zone of consideration for promotion.

In addition to eliminating much of the friction in brigade-level officer management, the proposed promotion timelines would have several advantages for the Army at large. First and foremost, this system would significantly reduce the time pressure currently associated with officer development. This reduction in time pressure would lead to a second advantage: reduced careerism among officers. Thirdly, individual officers would remain in position longer, developing greater expertise and enhancing the readiness of their particular unit. Finally, the Army would retain its ability to develop mid-level officers with both depth and breadth of experience. Each of these advantages enhances the overall viability of UFS by freeing officers to think more about unit cohesion and combat effectiveness and less about individual career management and advancement.

There are some obvious disadvantages to this proposal. First, slowed promotion necessarily means more officers will be required to serve longer. While longer officer careers are beneficial to the Army in many ways, they represent a significant change in expectations for the individual officer. Most military officers plan for a twenty-year military career and relish the opportunity for a second career in the civilian sector. Slowed promotions could force the Army to push its retirement eligibility point to twenty-five or thirty years. Such a change would be significant to the officer corps and could cause an increase in voluntary separation prior to retirement. Secondly, slowed promotion could create a general perception of reduced opportunity throughout the officer corps. Lieutenants with six years of commissioned service may long for the day when promotion to Captain occurred at the three-year mark. Likewise, majors at the twenty-year mark may yearn for the "good old days" when twenty years of service meant Lieutenant Colonel rank and retirement eligibility. Again, this comparison with the old system could create the perception of reduced opportunity and could result in increased voluntary attrition. Finally, under the proposed system, the commanders and staff officers at each level would be older than they are under the current system. As discussed in Chapter 3, this may not be a significant issue given the improved health and fitness of the officer corps and the changing conditions of the battlefield.

Certain changes would have to be made across other Army systems to mitigate the negative effects of the proposed change. First, the compensation tables would have to be changed to ensure the base pay for each officer is commensurate with his or her years of experience. The revised pay chart would reward officers more for their level of experience (measured in years of service) and less for increased rank. Second, to meet Army requirements for field grade officers, the retirement eligibility point would have to be changed. Under the proposed system, officers would not be selected for lieutenant colonel until twenty-one years of service—one year past the traditional retirement eligibility point. A promotion eligibility point of twenty-five years would ensure four years of service as lieutenant colonel prior to voluntary retirement. While detailed fiscal analysis would be required to validate this idea, such a measure would most likely ensure proper fill of the current structure for field grade officers. Elimination of the all-or-nothing retirement system and introduction of an up-or-stay system would complement the move of the promotion eligibility point. Finally, the Army would have to synchronize its military education system with this new promotion timeline. With less time pressure for individual officers, the education system would enjoy more flexibility in scheduling officers for school. Such a system may even increase opportunities for Advanced Civil Schooling, fellowships, and other educational experiences that are currently rare for the time-bound officer corps.

Slowing promotions and lengthening career timelines would provide direct and indirect support to the UFS initiative. It would make it easier for commanders in brigade combat teams to fully embrace and support the intent of Lifecycle management. These commanders could minimize personnel turbulence and maximize unit cohesion without fear of disadvantaging officers.

Option #3: Make Promotion Event-Driven

Under current laws and policies, officer promotion is clearly time-driven. The chrono-centric nature of the system provides little flexibility for officers, especially when combined with the up-or-out philosophy. Much flexibility could be gained by divorcing promotions from the bounds of time and tying it instead to critical events or decisions.

The promotion system could become event driven in one of two ways. First, officers could become eligible for promotion consideration only upon completion of critical branch-qualifying assignments. In other words, officers would enter the primary zone of consideration only when they had achieved the requisite level of professional experience required for the next grade. A second way to make promotion event-driven is to allow officers to self-select for promotion. Under this model, branch and career field proponents would provide guidelines for professional expertise at each grade. Once an officer deemed himself ready to compete for promotion, he could submit himself for consideration. Under either construct, the Army could retain the up-or-out character of the system by giving the officer a finite number of opportunities for selection. Likewise, the Army could easily incorporate an up-or-stay philosophy at any grade by allowing an unlimited number of considerations for promotion. Thus, under either option, promotion eligibility would be largely independent of time.

An event-driven promotion system would eliminate many of the UFS friction points within brigade combat teams. At every level, officers would have more time to achieve expertise. If the queue for critical jobs were long within a particular unit or at a certain installation, the officers in the queue would be less anxious as they awaited their turn. More importantly, the commanders of these officers would feel less pressure to violate the intent of UFS in order to move such officers quickly through the queue. Overall, the persistent career "time crunch" of the current system would dissipate. Freed from time pressure, unit cohesion and professional development would no longer be mutually exclusive.

Although this solution supports UFS well, it offers several significant disadvantages for the Army as a whole. First, the system will inevitably cause a slow in promotions. As described in Chapter 2, the closed nature of Lifecycle systems inevitably keeps officers in duty positions longer than under the Individual Replacement System. Whether officers self-select for promotion consideration or qualify for based on professional experience, it will take longer for officers to be ready of consideration. As discussed above, slowed promotions can cause reduced morale and increased voluntary attrition. Perhaps adjusted compensation tables could counterbalance this slowing of advancement.

A second disadvantage of event-driven promotions is the fact that managing such a system at Army level would be challenging at best. An event-driven promotion system would make it very difficult for Army-level personnel managers to maintain a constant fill of personnel structure at all levels. Personnel analysts at Human Resources Command use sophisticated models to predict officer attrition. These predictions allow them to manage officer promotion rates and to set officer accession levels—critical system functions that ensure proper officer fill throughout the Army. These personnel models rely heavily on the predicable flow of officer cohorts created by the time-driven system. Under an event-driven system, personnel managers would not be guaranteed a standard cohort of officers every year to backfill losses. It is completely possible that in a given year, only a small number of majors would self-select for the lieutenant colonel selection board, making it impossible to fill all vacancies in field grade structure. Of course, personnel managers have endured a similar management challenges in recent years caused by unprecedented (and unpredicted) levels of voluntary attrition at the lieutenant and captain level.[154] The event-driven promotion system would make such uncertainty the norm in personnel management.

To counter this management challenge, the Army would probably need to change its retirement system. The retirement eligibility point would need to be moved beyond the current twenty-year mark. Additionally, the Army would have to carefully manage voluntary retirements. The number of officers allowed to retire at a given point would be directly dependent upon the number of officers pushed upward by the event-driven promotion system. The Army might have to deny retirement to some officers pending upward advancement of junior cohorts. Such a policy would lead to significant discontent among senior field grade officers and their families, as was seen in 2003 with the wide use of Stop Loss to meet manpower requirements for Operation Iraqi Freedom.

Thus, while reducing friction in brigade combat teams, an event-driven promotion system would provide significant management challenges for the Army.

A Brief Comparison

Appendix A contains a tabular comparison of the three options. The table illustrates several things very clearly. First, of the three options, Option #1 (Up-or-Stay) provides the least direct support for UFS. The advantages of up-or-stay would be felt mostly by mid-level officers,

---

[154] Attrition for cohort Year Group 92, for example, was so high that given normal promotion rates, the cohort will never be able to fill all Army requirements. This information is based on the author's personal experience as an Assignment Officer at PERSCOM (now, Human Resources Command) when Year Group 92 went before the selection board for promotion to Major. At that time, the author was told by PERSCOM analysts that in order to meet all field grade requirements, the Army would have to promote 120% of Year Group 92 officers. Year Groups 91, 93, and 94 have suffered similar un-forecasted attrition rates.

and these officers would experience only indirect relief of timeline and career pressures. Option #3 (Event-Driven Promotion) does much to mitigate the friction points of UFS, but it, too, fails to address many of the friction points directly. Third, Option #2 (Lengthened Career Timelines) significantly reduces or mitigates many of the UFS friction points for company- and field-grade officers. Finally, there are at least three friction points that will remain unaffected by any of the options.

While Option #2 (Lengthened Career Timelines) appears to provide the best support to an Army-wide shift to UFS, it also represents the most significant shift in mindset for the officer corps. As discussed above, slowed promotions translate directly to longer career and later retirements for officers. Such a notion conflicts violently with two deep-seated cultural norms: the twenty-year retirement point and the opportunity for a second career in the civilian sector. Likewise, slowed promotion rates hearken back to pre-World War II days of stagnation and limited upward mobility. The perceived reduction in opportunity may pose morale problems for the officer corps.

The Way Ahead

The options presented in this chapter provide a starting point for personnel planners who wish to ensure the longevity of UFS. Obviously, each option requires further development, testing and analysis. Likewise, the feasibility, suitability, and acceptability of each must be evaluated in the context of other Army systems to include the Officer Personnel Management System Three (OPMS3) and the Officer Education System. Sophisticated modeling is essential to the testing process. Thus, Army Operational Research and Systems Analysis (ORSA) specialists should begin work immediately on the development of the required models.

The options presented here may not be beneficial to officers of every branch and every career field. UFS is designed to improve unit cohesion in combat units and in critical support units. Thus, any measure to alleviate the friction of UFS will be optimized for members of such units—perhaps at the expense of other officers. The Army must re-examine its "one-size-fits-all" approach to officer promotions. A decentralized, non-standardized approach to officer promotions may better support the success of UFS while ensuring the health and vitality of the officer corps as a whole.

Each of the proposed options would require a significant alteration of Title 10, USC. History demonstrates clearly that legal change takes a long time. If changing the officer promotion system is critical to the long-term success of UFS, then the Army must immediately begin working towards that goal. Temporary Congressional authorizations and Department of Defense policy adjustments could provide short-term help, but fundamental changes to the officer promotion system require the passage of a DOPMA equivalent. The Army must decide on an option and move quickly to provide the required support for UFS.

Senior Army leaders have wasted no time in enacting the UFS initiative. In three years, most of the brigade combat teams in the Army will fall under the Lifecycle management model.[155] Unfortunately, the current promotion system will force commanders in those units to choose between unit cohesion and individual officer career progression. A change in the officer promotion system could make cohesion and officer advancement compatible—or at least, ensure they are not mutually exclusive. Without such a change, the bold manning initiative will crumble under the weight of long-standing systemic and cultural norms. Delayed action in changing officer promotions will spell eventual doom for UFS.

CHAPTER FIVE: CONCLUSIONS AND RECOMMENDATIONS

Since its earliest days, the United States Army has wrestled with the challenges of manning its formations. In peace and war, commanders and their adjutants general have sought the elusive balance between bureaucratic efficiency and combat effectiveness, between centralization and decentralization, and between needs of the individual soldier and needs of the unit. The UFS initiative is the latest manifestation of these persistent dilemmas.

This monograph began with the assumption that UFS is a feasible, acceptable, and suitable solution for the Army and that it will be implemented Army-wide according to published timelines. There is still some question about whether UFS creates significant improvements in unit cohesion and whether this cohesion leads to improved combat effectiveness. However, that debate is for another forum. This investigation assumes that the success of UFS is good for the Army and that its success is so critical as to warrant significant systemic and cultural change.

It is clear that UFS will cause significant friction for officer management at the brigade-level and below. Chapter 2 described eight friction points for lieutenant through colonel; additional friction points will inevitably develop upon implementation of the program. Each one represents a conflict between individual officer development and unit cohesion, between the needs of the one and the needs of the many, and between the way things have always been done and the way things must be done in the future. If the Army fails to mitigate or eliminate this friction, officers will "take matters into their own hands," exempting themselves from the provisions of UFS. The draft regulations for UFS allow just enough "wiggle room" for commanders to violate the intent of the program in the interest of maintaining the norms of officer management. The history of past unit manning initiatives tells us that if officers are not included in the effort, the program will fail. Without Army-level efforts to reduce friction, UFS will meet a similar fate.

The Army has recognized the need for complementary changes in regulations, policies, and procedures to support UFS. A robust effort to revamp OPMS3 is already underway at

---

[155] U.S. Department of the Army, Human Resources Command. "Life Cycle Management." Briefing Slide. Alexandria, VA.: 2004. The current schedule implements Lifecycle Management in three

Human Resources Command. Such change is desperately needed and must be implemented as soon as possible. However, there is only so much personnel managers can do with OPMS3 before they run into the "DOPMA wall." Any changes they make to the personnel management system must fall within the bounds of Title 10 as set forth by DOPMA. These bounds provide limited flexibility to an Army trying to make a fundamental shift in its manning paradigm.

Senior Army leaders must recognize that DOPMA is out of synch with the realities of the current environment. At its foundation are old assumptions of questionable validity in the post-Cold War and post-9/11 world. Its scaffolding features implementation principles that maximize bureaucratic efficiency at the expense of unit cohesion. DOPMA is ripe for change.

This monograph proposed three options that would mitigate or eliminate UFS friction points. The first is one of the favorite panaceas among contemporary writers: the adoption of an up-or-stay promotion system. This system would provide macro-level support to the implementation of UFS. It would do little to alleviate the friction at brigade-level and below. Primarily, up-or-stay would mitigate the long-term, negative effects of UFS.

The second option features the lengthening of officer career timelines and the synchronization of these timelines with personnel lifecycles. This option would eliminate or mitigate most of the friction points in brigade combat teams, and it would provide greater long-term flexibility by offering additional opportunities for promotion consideration. Inevitable side-effect of this option would be lengthened careers and an older officer corps. To implement such an option, the Army would have to make significant adjustments to its compensation tables and its retirement system.

The third option features the adoption of an event-driven promotion system. Such a system would divorce officer promotion from strict timelines. According to one variation, officers would compete for promotion only upon achieving a requisite level of experience. A

BCTs in FY04, six BCTs in FY05, ten in FY06, thirteen in FY07, five in FY08, and two in FY09.

second variation allows officers to self-select for promotion. Like Option #2, an event-driven promotion system would undoubtedly lead to longer officer careers, older officers, and a changed retirement system. Officer flow in an event-driven system is not as predictable as under the current system. Therefore, Army personnel managers would find themselves particularly challenged under this system to maintain consistent fill of Army officer billets.

Each solution requires refinement and further development. Such refinement is beyond the realm of academia; it is time for the personnel experts to take on this challenge. The optimum solution for the Army may be a combination of all three options presented in this paper, but one cannot really know until experts conduct detailed systems analysis to test potential changes. Regardless, any one of the options is better than doing nothing.

There are several things the Army must do to ensure the long-term success of UFS and the health of the officer corps. First and foremost, the Army must commit wholeheartedly to the concept of unit manning. Senior Leaders have endorsed the concept, but buy-in is scarce at the level of implementation. Skeptics have performed their own mental analysis, and they understand clearly that UFS will change everything about the way the Army manages soldiers and officers. They also understand that few other changes have been enacted in conjunction with UFS to make the radical changes palatable. Army leaders can reassure the critics by conducting formal, scientific modeling to predict the second- and third- order effects of UFS. To date, no such testing has been done. After careful analysis, the Army must clearly articulate for officers and soldiers what friction they will experience and more importantly, what the organization is doing to mitigate these effects. At least then, commanders can support the initiative knowing that there is an Army-level plan to deal with the consequences.

Secondly, the Army must provide strict policies and implementation guidance to ensure UFS is enacted in accordance with its stated intent. The draft regulations for UFS provide commanders significant leeway in managing officers within brigade combat teams. According to the rules, commanders can easily violate the intent of the program, breaking the short-lived bonds of vertical cohesion in combat units from platoon to brigade. Prioritizing unit cohesion over individual officer advancement requires a significant cultural change for the officer corps. Army commanders may need more directive policies to help them make this cultural leap.

Thirdly, the Army must recognize that a change to the officer promotion system is fundamental to the success of UFS, and it must move quickly to develop the framework for an improved system. To create a foundation for this new framework, the Army must bring the tacit assumptions of the officer promotion system to the surface, and these must be examined and re-evaluated under the light of the current environment. With sound assumptions and implementation principles, Army leaders can forge the details of a new officer promotion system. While a basic concept can be developed in isolation, the specifics of any promotion system must take into account all interrelated Army systems. Experts in Operational Research and Systems Analysis (ORSA) must develop models that replicate the complex Army systems and illustrate the effects of UFS. Psychologists and behavioral scientists must determine how the changing paradigm in officer management will change the nature of the officer corps. In developing a framework for a new promotion system, the Army must ensure a holistic approach that considers the breadth of personnel, training, and support systems.

Once a framework is developed, the Army must press hard for Congressional action. This will be no easy task. Not only must senior Army leaders convince key members of Congress that DOPMA needs adjustment, but they must also demonstrate that many of its assumptions and principles are invalid and counter-productive. Undoubtedly, Army proposals will not meet the needs of the other services. If Congress maintains the principle of inter-service standardization in officer promotions, then senior army leaders will face the daunting task of gaining inter-service consensus. Regardless, changes to Title 10 will take a long time, and any delay is detrimental to the success of UFS.

In the mean time, the Army must develop a plan for intermediate provisions to "bridge-the-gap" until a new promotion system can be approved and implemented. Temporary authorizations from Congress, Department of Defense policy changes, and Army regulatory changes may provide some flexibility to commanders in brigade combat teams. However, such temporary measures should not be mistaken for long-term solutions. If the Army wants a permanent change to its manning paradigm, then it must invest in permanent measures to ensure the success of such a change.

For the thirteenth time in the last century, the Army is attempting a fundamental shift in its manning paradigm. Organizational culture and bureaucratic inertia present formidable obstacles for successful adoption of UFS. If Army leaders are serious about making UFS a successful part of Army personnel management, then they must commit to fundamental changes in the way we promote officers. Without such total commitment to change, UFS will be immortalized in the history books as "another good idea that just didn't work."

APPENDIX A: COMPARISON OF OPTIONS

	Friction Point	Options #1: Up-or-Stay	Option #2: Lengthen Career Timelines	Option #3: Event-Driven Promotions
Lieutenants	Reduction in assignment options for individual officer	~	~	~
	Splitting LT population into "haves" and "have nots"	~	M	M
	Individual LT cannot gain breadth of experience through multiple cascading jobs within BCT	~	X	X
	CDRs challenged to fill traditional senior LT positions at beginning of "Reset" phase (all incoming lieutenants are inexperienced, no cascading levels of experience)	~	X	X
	All LTs will pin-on CPT before end of lifecycle	~	X	X
Captains	Individual CPT cannot gain breadth of experience through multiple cascading jobs within BCT	~	X	X
	Not all CPTs will have opportunity to command within a BCT during its lifecycle	~	M	M
	CDRs challenged to fill commands at beginning of "Reset" phase (all incoming CPTs are inexperienced, no cascading levels of experience)	~	X	M
	CDRs forced to choose between branch-qualifying maximum number of captains and unit readiness	M	M	M
	Reduced production of BQ CPTs	~	~	~
Majors	Long queue and time crunch for BQ before LTC board	M	M	M
	Reduced production of BQ MAJs	~	~	~
LTCs and COLs	Reduced Command Opportunity	M	M	M
Legend: X = Friction Point **SIGNIFICANTLY REDUCED** by option M = Friction Point **MITIGATED** by option				

BIBLIOGRAPHY

Books

Henderson, William Darryl. *The Hollow Army: How the U.S. Army is Oversold and Undermanned.* New York: Greenwood Press, 1990.

Straub, Christopher C. *The Unit First: Keeping the Promise of Cohesion.* Washington, DC: National Defense University Press, 1988.

Vandergriff, Donald E. *The Path to Victory: America's Army and the Revolution in Human Affairs.* Presidio: Presidio Press, 2002.

Rostker, Bernard, Harry Thie, James Lacy, Jennifer Kawata, and Susanna Purnell. *The Defense Officer Personnel Management Act of 1980: A Retrospective Assessment.* Santa Monica: Rand, 1993.

Rostker, Bernard. "Changing the Officer Personnel System." In *Filling the Ranks: Transforming the U.S. Military Personnel System,* edited by Cindy Williams, 146-166. Cambridge: MIT Press, 2004.

Stanley-Mitchell, Elizabeth A. "The Military Profession and Intangible Rewards for Service." In *Filling the Ranks: Transforming the U.S. Military Personnel System,* edited by Cindy Williams, 93-118. Cambridge: MIT Press, 2004.

Strawn, Thomas M. "The War for Talent in the Private Sector." In *Filling the Ranks: Transforming the U.S. Military Personnel System,* edited by Cindy Williams, 69-91. Cambridge: MIT Press, 2004.

Williams, Cindy, ed. Filling the Ranks: Transforming the U.S. Military Personnel System. Cambridge: MIT Press, 2004.

U.S. Government Publications

U.S. Congress. House. *Defense Officer Personnel Management Act.* 96th Cong., 2d sess., 1980. H.Rep. 96-1462.

U.S. Army Human Resources Command. *Unit Focused Stabilization Playbook (Final Coordinating Draft).* Alexandria, VA.: 2004.

U.S. Department of the Army. *AR 600-XX, Force Stabilization (Draft).* Washington, D.C.: 2004.

_____. *AR 600-8-29, Officer Promotion.* Washington, D.C.: 2004.

_____. *AR 600-83, The New Manning System—COHORT Unit Replacement System.* Washington, D.C.: 1986.

_____. *AR 614-1, The U.S. Army Replacement System.* Washington, D.C.: 1969.

_____. *DA Pam 600-3, Commissioned Officer Development and Career Management.* Washington, D.C.: 1998.

U.S. Department of the Army, Committee on Classification of Personnel in the Army. *The Personnel System of the United States Army, Vol. I: History of the Personnel System.* Washington, D.C.: 1919.

U.S. Department of Defense. *Department of Defense Instruction Number 1320.13: Commissioned Officer Promotion Reports (COPRs) and Procedures.* Washington, D.C.: 21 June, 1996.

_____. *Department of Defense Instruction Number 1320.14: Commissioned Officer Promotion Program Procedures.* Washington, D.C.: 24 September, 1996.

Articles

Alford, Eli T.S. "Implementing a Unit Manning System." *Military Review* LXXXIX, No. 1(Jan-Feb 2004): 54-60.

Bell, William F. "The Impact of Policies on Organizational Values and Culture." http://usafa.af.mil/jscope/JSCOPE99/Bell99.html (accessed November 12, 2004).

Brownlee, Les and Peter J. Schoomaker. "Serving a Nation at War: A Campaign Quality Army with Joint and Expeditionary Capabilities." *Parameters* XXXIV, No. 2 (Summer 2004): 5-23.

Elton, Robert M. "A Unit Manning System for the Objective Force: Recommendations for Vital Changes in Army Manning Policies." With the collaboration of Joseph Trez. https://www.stabilization.army.mil/Research_items/manning_items (accessed October 8 2004) Oct 2002.

Gayton, Jamie S. "Have We Finally Found the Manning Holy Grail?" *Military Review LXXXIV, No. 2* (Mar-Apr 2004): 17-20.

Mahnken, Thomas G. and James R. Fitzsimonds. "Tread-Heads or Technophiles? Army Officer Attitudes Toward Transformation." *Parameters* XXXIV, No. 2 (Summer 2004): 57-72.

Military Times. "ARMY Announces Force Stabilization Initiative," February 10, 2004, http://www.military-times.info/article_125.html (accessed 4 August 2004).

Vandergriff, Donald A. "Unit Manning Will Benefit the Many." D.N.I Website at http://www.d-n-i.net/fcs/vandergriff_unit_manning.htm.

Theses

Lauderdale, Larry. "Should Promotion to Captain within the United States Army become Decentralized?" Masters Thesis, Naval Post Graduate School, 1983.

Miscellaneous

Complin, Graham. "A Wasted Investment? The Career Management of Royal Signals Young Officers." In *Human Resource Management in the British Armed Forces: Investing in the Future,* ed. Alex Alexandrou, Richard Bartle, and Richard Holmes, 29-66. London: Frank Cass Publishers, 2001.

Hernandez, Rhett. "OPMD Update for CGSC Class AY 04-05." Briefing, Command and General Staff College, Fort Leavenworth, KS, September 8, 2004.

Sanders, Dave and Mike McGinnis. "Unit Manning the Army's Combat Brigades." West Point: United States Military Academy Operations Research Center of Excellence, 2003.

Schirmer, Peter, Dina G. Levy, Harry J. Thie, Joy S. Moini, Margaret C. Harrell, Kimberly Curry, Kevin Brancato, and Megan Abbott. "New Paths to Success: Determining Career Alternatives for Field-Grade Officers." Santa Monica: RAND Corporation, 2004. http://www.rand.org/publications/MG/MG117.html. (accessed September 2, 2004).

Thie, Harry J., Mark Berends, Roger A. Brown, Rudolph H. Ehrenberg, Jr., Ann Flanagan, Claire Mitchell Levy, and William W. Taylor. "Future Career Management Systems for U.S. Military Officers." Santa Monica: RAND Corporation, 1994. http://www.rand.org/publications/MR/MR470/. (accessed November 9, 2004)

Tillson, John C. F. "Reducing the Impact of Tempo." Alexandria: Institute for Defense Analyses, 1999. http://www.d-n-i.net/fcs/tillson_tempo.pdf. (accessed September 2, 2004).

U.S. Army Human Resources Command. "OPMS3 Council of Colonels 31 Aug – 2 Sep 04." Slide presentation. https://www.perscom.army.mil/opfamdd/LDD3_Hotwash.pps (accessed November 12, 2004).

U.S. Department of the Army. "Force Stabilization Homepage" https://www.stabilization.army.mil (accessed July 28, 2004).

_____. "Force Stabilization: Key Elements of Force Stabilization" https://www.stabilization.army.mil/Overview/Key%20Elements.htm (accessed October 10, 2004).

_____. "Force Stabilization: Leader Information Briefing" https://www.stabilization.army.mil/Briefings/Ldr%20Info%20Brief.ppt (accessed October 8, 2004).

_____. "Force Stabilization: Policy Adjustments" https://www.stabilization.army.mil/Products_items/policy_changes.htm (accessed October 8, 2004).

_____. "Force Stabilization: What You Can Expect" https://www.stabilization.army.mil/Overview/What%20you%20can%20expect.htm (accessed October 8, 2004).

White, Jeffrey S. "Getting to the Business of Officer Personnel Management." Strategy Research Project, U.S. Army War College, 2000.